No Guts, No Story

No Guts, No Story

*A Tale of Courage and Success
from the Heartland*

Barb Pitcock

SelectBooks, Inc.
New York

This edition published by SelectBooks, Inc. For information address
SelectBooks, Inc., New York, N.Y. 10003.

First Edition

ISBN 978-1-59079-207-0

Library of Congress Cataloging-in-Publication Data

Pitcock, Barbara, 1971-
No guts, no story : tale of courage and success from the heartland /
Barbara Pitcock. — 1st ed.
p. cm.
Summary: "A woman from a small town in Kansas describes her triumphs and
setbacks as she achieves both personal happiness and widely recognized
success as a self-made millionaire in a home-based network marketing
business"—Provided by publisher.
ISBN 978-1-59079-207-0 (pbk. : alk. paper)
1. Multilevel marketing—United States. 2. Success in business—United States.
I. Title.
HF5415.126.P565 2010
381'.1—dc22
[B]
                                    2010009023

Interior text design by Kathleen Isaksen

Printed in the United States of America

10 9 8 7 6 5 4 3 2 1

*This book is dedicated to all of the
ordinary people with extra-ordinary dreams,*

*and to my husband, Dave,
and our three children,
Brooklyn, Chance, and Kali Anne*

Contents

Foreword

WHEN I FIRST READ the title of *No Guts, No Story,* I thought it was a typo from the infamous quote by my colleague and friend Dexter Yager, "No Guts, No Glory," but after reading this manuscript, it is very clear why Barb has this unique title and why this book will impact the lives of its readers. I believe stories and great story-tellers can change your life. We've learned some of life's most valuable lessons from childhood fables, stories from friends and family, and now for me, many inspirational messages from *No Guts, No Story.*

Wouldn't it be nice if our lives read as a fairy-tale book? How enjoyable would our lives be if we had little-to-no havoc, few disappointments and defeats, and happy times to forever remember? What if our only problem was trying to find contentment and live 'happily ever after'? Well as strange as it might seem, I believe we lead fairy-tale lives, full of adventure (otherwise disguised as challenges), packed with villains (also known as naysayers), and happiness (which is sweeter after reflecting about personal victories).

Imagine if you died, only to realize you never really lived and in no way scraped the surface of your true potential? That would be devastating. But I found that this is the reality for most people because they are afraid to do as Mother Teresa said which is to be a pencil in the hands of God. Most people don't want to shake up their lives to pursue something different and against the status-quo. That's why I believe the graveyard is the richest place in the world, because many shy away from writing a new chapter in their lives.

Some don't want guts or a story. Barb's title is so significant to me, because it took guts for me to believe I could earn millions of dollars, change people's lives, and be named one of the top five speakers in the world, considering my grim, impoverish circumstances. It takes guts to believe you can beat incurable illnesses, but many do. And it took guts for Barb's husband to spend $1000 of borrowed money to start a new business when creditors were their only "friends" because they called so often, but he did. And with that leap of faith, they have written many new chapters in their lives and have touched and inspired the lives many others.

No Guts, No Story is laugh-out-loud funny. Barb is honest and transparent. The writing is bold and vivid, not a bunch of self-help fluff, but many real stories, with lessons to apply in many areas of your life today.

Les Brown
www.LesBrown.com

Acknowledgments

WRITING THIS BOOK has been a project of mine for the last ten years and a dream that I always knew some day would become a reality. There were days I would sit and write when I was full of energy, and other days my tank was definitely on E, for empty. My mentor told me that one day my story would have an impact on other people's lives, so through every adversity and every setback I would smile and say "This is going to make a great story!" Sometimes I would cry and say, "We will laugh about this someday ... but not now!"

My husband and my best friend, David Pitcock, is the one I am thankful for every day. He made my life complete, and as you will read, he changed my life and continues to, every day that I am with him. My children have been a never ending inspiration to me, and along the way I would envision the legacy I could leave them, if I could just complete this book. Brooklyn, Chance, and Kali—I thank God every day that He blessed me with such wonderful children. You are the story of my life, and because of you I woke up everyday with a new dream, a new energy, and the strength to persevere even in the toughest of times.

I could list a thousand people who have helped me become the person I am today, but it all began with my Mom and Dad who brought me into this world and taught me how to dream every day that they were together. They taught me to work and persevere and that anything in life worth having is worth working for. They never handed me anything. They taught me how to earn it, and for that I am thankful. My dad taught me strength, and after many years of resentment and anger directed toward him, I learned to be understanding and forgiving.

To my Grandma Mills who always told me she was proud of me, I was beautiful, and I had so much talent … Grandma, it was the memory of your praise and pride in me that helped me see the person I could become, instead of the unattractive, untalented, freckled-face, little redhead I saw staring at me in the mirror. Thank you for the foundation you gave me as a child.

Mom, you taught me how to become someone's hero—and you are mine. I know that my sisters, Traci and Lori, and brothers, Mark and Jeremy, would agree. There is no mountain too high, and the bond we share is truly a gift. That bond has given me the strength to come out of every adversity even stronger than before, and for that I am thankful.

To the many family members who have surrounded me with love and support and taught me what family means—there are so many of you, and you are my most valued asset.

I want to thank the many faces in the crowd that have come to me with tears in their eyes after each speaking engagement and told me that this story changed their life. You gave my life meaning and inspired me to share the entire truth and, to hold nothing back in the hope that what I shared would impact others.

I want to thank my assistant, Laura Boxberger, and Cindy Pitcock, my mother-in-law, who spent many hours reading and giving me their thoughts and suggestions; the story is yours to read.

Writing this book helped me survive many events in my life, and kept me focused on the faith I had deep inside me even at times when I had doubt creeping in. I thank God for the many experiences He has given me: the strength to survive, the lessons I have learned, and the people He has put in my path. I am thankful for so many mentors who gave me words of wisdom, encouragement, and had belief in me when nobody else thought it could be done. Thank you to Kevin Trudeau who taught my husband and me how to dream when we had nothing, and transformed us into giants in the industry of Direct Sales through his life-changing training and system. Today I am still using those principles of success and finding my true "bliss." The great Jim Rohn, Charlie Tremendous Jones, Les Brown, Anthony Robbins, Brian Tracy, and Desi Williamson gave me the personal development tools through their books and audio tapes that I literally wore out until it became a reality in my life. Without them, I would have quit.

Thank You, God, for the grace you have given me. Along the way there were people who came into my life for only a short time and then they were gone, but the conversations, the inspiration and the lessons I learned from them, will be with me forever. I am thankful for the ability to be teachable and never stop learning, growing, and becoming the person that God intended me to be. We are all "Destined for Greatness," but to reach that greatness many friends, family, and mentors play a part along the way.

I've heard people say "It's the journey, not the destination." ... It is the journey I am so thankful for.

Introduction

GROWING UP IN THE SMALL TOWN of Russell, Kansas with only five stop lights and less than 2,500 people, I guess you could say we were a bit sheltered. My parents raised five of us in a three bedroom house where the girls shared a canopy bed and the boys had bunks across the hall.

Until I was about twelve I remember loving my bedroom at Grandma's house where I spent most days and many nights. Grandma and Grandpa Mills were much like my mom and dad in that they worked around the clock and actually were partners with my parents in rental properties and an R.V. park.

I'd spend my summers mowing the campground or cleaning out vacant mobile homes so that the next tenants could move in. There was always something to be done and not much time to get bored. Television was almost prohibited and playtime was a reward that you got after you finished all your chores, did your piano, baton, and Sunday school lessons, or completed a project that Grandma or my parents had started.

After my grandmother lost her battle with cancer in 1982 my world was never quite the same. She had been my rock, showing me unconditional love and giving me the spiritual foundation that I didn't understand was so important when I was a young girl. Little did I know this foundation would help me survive so much that the future had in store for her little red-headed, freckled-faced girl she called "Barbie."

At the age of twelve I had to grow up. Without Grandma my mother needed me to help her with the children as she continued to work with my dad running their businesses and making a living for our family. I was just a kid raising kids, and like any teenager I hated my parents and thought they didn't know anything.

The work ethic that I learned was something that few in our small town understood. There was no time for sports—nor would my mom and dad have stopped to come and watch me participate. They drove two semi-trucks and owned a food distribution company, along with a grocery store that was about a half-hour's drive north of Russell. They also owned the putt-putt golf course that was at the campground. I learned to run the cash register, greet people, and run the front of many of their businesses before most kids were able to stay alone and baby sit.

My parents were also born and raised in our small town, so they knew most everyone there. This made it very hard to get too mischievous because anything I did would get back to them by morning. It wasn't as if I had a lot of time to get into trouble, but like any kid, I created my fair share. I thought I knew everything and I became very hateful and mouthy, which led to many beatings from my father. I criticized him for things that I felt were wrong and would remind him that his children were not my kids to raise. I loved my younger brothers and sisters, Lori, Mark, Traci, and Jeremy, and cared a great deal for them. They taught me so much about motherhood, but that didn't take away the resentment I had as a kid when all of my friends were playing softball or swimming at the pool. I usually took the kids with me to the pool to play with them just so I could see my friends there. Today I am thankful for the lessons I was taught, but back then I always thought I was underprivileged.

There were no cell phones then, so the base that sat in our kitchen was a way to call Mom and Dad on the CB in case of emergency. I could hear them update their locations and talk about different things about the business as they traveled their routes. They travelled several hours outside of our home town, delivering milk, dairy products, and frozen food items to restaurants, stores, and schools. By the time I was in eighth grade I would cook, clean, do the laundry, get the kids to preschool or day care before I went to school, and pick them up after school to soon start the routine over again. I learned a lot about responsibility, hard work, setting goals, and making sacrifices. I would need those survival lessons, because I had no idea what it would be like when my mom and I were on our own. One day in May during my senior year in high school, my dad made a decision to leave. Much like my grandmother did, he taught me many lessons and then disappeared. After this, my feelings about being so mistreated and the feelings of hatred toward my parents changed. I learned to love my mom and became very close to her as I watched her survive as a single mom of five with no child support. It would be several years before we discovered where our father was.

This book begins in 1992 when I was a young woman trying to sort out my life and what my destiny was. Wanting to put my thoughts on paper, I began my journals after I married and my husband and I began our entrepreneurial journey through the next ten years. I realized that what I wanted to say might never be published, but hoped that my strong faith and energy would lead me to tell my story. Hopefully it would inspire many others to go where they have not been before, and to conquer and achieve what they have not seen in their own lives. In the end I hoped my experiences would give them the faith, the strength, and the belief to achieve their destinies.

I believe that if this story is read by many and becomes a bestseller in bookstores all over the world, it will be because it is a true experience. It exposes the same feelings that so many people have but don't ordinarily have the courage or opportunity to share with others—the pain, the fear, the anger, the sorrow, or the feelings about victory over difficulties that they experience. God is real, and so are all of the emotions we have to experience in this world. Along the way our feelings about our choices will be ours to live with.

I hope you are inspired by the adversities that I have overcome and that you will find yourself gaining the strength, wisdom, and belief to help you achieve your dreams in whatever you pursue in life. Whether you are struggling with difficult problems of your parents' divorce, or cancer, a suicide, bankruptcy, or even something as seemingly small as a low self-esteem, I believe that there is someone out there who has been where you are. I believe that someone can overcome adversity and rise above the pain, the fear, the anger, the sorrow and the doubt, only to grow stronger. In order for things to get better ... YOU have to get better, and I believe that you will get better as you read these pages and can see yourself able to overcome obstacles. As long as you don't quit, your failure is not final. Keep learning, growing, and striving to become that person you were created to be—the person that is destined for greatness!

My wish is that you will become the Victor—not the Victim. I hope that you will take all of your excuses not to succeed and make them the reasons to succeed. You will have to have some Guts, or you will never have a Story! Your story can change the lives of many in ways you have never dreamed.

No Guts, No Story

1

I Was Lost

I HEARD SIRENS as I pulled into the old Safeway grocery store parking lot. Evidently the cops had been called after a teenage fight broke out in the middle of Main Street. When I drove past the fight in my slick little red convertible, I heard the boys whistling at me as I caught a glance of the heart throb of Russell, Kansas starting another fight on that little downtown Main Street. I had no interest at all in the guys who whistled. I had too many responsibilities in my life to join the group of people my age who were having a party on the block that night. Going to those kind of parties had never excited me that much.

Instead, I sat in my car in the parking lot, shaking and praying for God to give me the strength to get through this difficult time. A lot had happened in the last twenty-four hours, and I was just trying to figure it all out.

On that Friday night in August of 1992, although I was only twenty-two years old, I felt much older. It had been ten years since my first date in seventh grade with the boy who was now my fiancé. I had believed for a long time that he would someday love me as much as I believed I loved him. And now it seemed that my dreams and plans for our life together were shattered.

I had again worked a full day at my beauty salon. After that I decided to take my little brothers and sisters to the Odin Rodeo, a small town rodeo just outside of my home town.

That was one of the first nights in weeks I hadn't gone straight home exhausted from work. I felt that I needed to spend some time with my sister and brother, Traci and Jeremy, who were just five and seven years old. It had never dawned on me that I should go straight home after the rodeo. Instead I left the rodeo with the children and my friend Tina to take a ride in the country. We went in search of one of those dream homes we had heard about, a mansion where a successful couple lived with their two children.

I was young with big dreams and a lot of ambition, and had recently joined a direct selling/networking company with cosmetics products. It made sense to me, since I owned a hair salon, that I might as well get an extra stream of income coming in. After all, I looked at the houses some of those people lived in and the cars they drove—not to mention the photos that showed their husbands close to them with a pile of kids and grandkids. That is all I ever dreamed of, and I wanted what they had!

I have never been too good at finding my way around in the country and I became lost. Soon it was 12:45AM. The evening at the rodeo seemed like a good idea until I got home and the man I planned to marry flew into a rage because I came home a bit late. I will never forget what happened when I pulled into the driveway of the beautiful brick home that I was leasing. I could see the cars lined up, and there was a crowd on my porch. Suddenly this violent man, my fiancé, was beating on my windshield like an outraged animal. When I got out of the car and approached the front door, he gave me a swift kick with his hiking boot right in my back. I ran to the house to quickly change my clothes, crying and wishing that no one was around. My sister Lori had tried to protect me by standing between us. And I thought about my little brother Mark, just ten years old, who adored this man I lived with. I guess you could say he was his role model since he never had a dad at home.

I was the oldest of five, and I had helped my mother raise the other four children. It was important to me to protect the children from the kind of thing they were now seeing, and keep them safe. I tried to calm down my fiancé as he screamed, "Where have you been?" And I wondered, "What is the big deal?" I thought it was the whiskey talking. Although I had been heartbroken a lot, I hadn't been physically hit since I was in high school. I always said I would rather be beaten than cheated on. At least the temporary pain would go away, but now I was rethinking my statement.

Although I sat at home a lot of empty nights wondering where my fiancé was, this was the first night in months I had done something I wanted to do. "Who were you with?" he screamed. As I ran for the door, he continued to threaten me. I ran out the door and didn't stop running until I got to the campground about a mile away where my mother lived. I cried as I ran, and I wished things were different. I wished he loved me and was faithful to me. I also wished I looked like so many of the other beautiful girls I caught him with after work or at the lake where they all hung out on the weekends. I thought I would never find anyone else, especially in Russell, Kansas, and I couldn't leave Russell when my family was there, my salon was there, and I had built up a successful dance school. I just always hoped he would change, but he never did.

I dreamed of the wedding I would have in a huge church, the children I would raise, and the nice things I would be able to give them if I continued to work extremely hard. I had watched my mother raise the five of us after my father had left, and all I dreamed of was a happy family and a husband who believed in me.

My sister Lori drove quickly in her Jeep convertible to Mom's house. She was worried about me and told me we should go for a drive. I didn't want to be negative, and I didn't want her to know just how much of a jerk he was. There was no hiding the broken mirror and the cracked windshield of my car, nor the boot print on my back. She was very well aware that I was headed down the same road my mom had gone … young, in love, and struggling in vain to keep a man faithful to her no matter how much she loved him. We both cried, and we listened to our favorite country audio cassette, Alabama, singing into the wind as we drove down the dark streets.

Lori pulled into an old church parking lot, blaring our music next to an old classmate of hers, named Scott, who had his Metallica Metal on full volume. His car was bouncing from the bass, and he didn't even notice us. I, being the friendly older sister, jumped out of the Jeep and onto his bumper until he and his friend noticed us. It was then that he made his famous comment we'd always remember, "What is that crap you are listening to?" he asked. "It's the good stuff," we replied. Knowing this kid's brother Dave was a professional bull-rider and an old classmate of mine, I just shook my head at his blaring heavy metal and smiled. As we drove off, I said to him, "We'd probably get along better with your brother." My sister Lori made a comment about how Scott had been her first love. Boy, she said, he had really changed, going from his cowboy boots to heavy metal, but she thought his older brother Dave, was still pretty fine. I ignored her comments and laughed. I had my eyes on only one thing, and it was the one thing I couldn't have. I tried so hard to make something wrong a right, and I had no idea what God had in store for me.

I didn't know that Scott took my comment about having more in common with his brother seriously until several days later when Dave called me for a hair cut and told me he had a proposition for me. I laughed it off, postponed his appointment for a haircut, and told him I was pretty much married. I did agree to get back to him. I knew he was also engaged. Or I had heard he was, and the one thing I didn't ever want to experience again was a guy who cheated. My sister Lori, stood at the counter in my salon with her jaw hitting the floor as she overheard my phone call. She questioned my reply to him as she mocked my behavior, muttering under her breath, "Oh no, I'm not interested in a nice guy. I'm going to get off work and go to the lake to see how many girls my boyfriend has loaded in the boat that I'm paying for!" I told her to shut-up, and we loaded up in her Jeep. We hauled all of the dirty towels from the salon home to wash and we cleaned up the chaos left from the party the night before.

I finally had time to go to the lake later that afternoon. I saw that my fiancé was out in our boat that was full of people and I was the only one sober. I stayed on the beach for a while, and then went home and waited until 8:00 or 9:00PM for him to come home. It was then that I got in my car and drove off, not knowing that I would never again have to ask for permission from my fiancé for anything.

No matter how hard I prayed, it seemed that this relationship just wasn't meant to be. Everyone always had their advice, but none of it was what I wanted to hear. My mentors in my present company told me to find someone new. My grandmother, who raised me, would have rolled over in her grave had she known about the lifestyle I was living. More important than that, I knew in my heart my relationship with him was going nowhere, but I wanted to be loved. Ten years of dating, 22 years old, with a house, a salon of my own, a dance school, and four little brothers and sisters depending on me, I had to suck it up.

I had also been in the direct sales company for about four years and had personally sponsored a lot of people to work for the company. I had to keep a positive face, because they depended on me. I didn't want them to know it wasn't good at home. I would listen to the company's training tapes and be so encouraged in my work, but at other times when I really needed to listen to them in order to remain motivated, I didn't have the strength to listen. A sad love song was more appealing as I basked in the misery of my broken heart.

I fumbled for a cassette while parked in the Safeway grocery alley parking lot—running from it all! I looked in the mirror of that little

Lebaron Convertible, and I could see the people in the parking lot a block away. Everyone seemed so free and with no worries. They were just young kids out having a good time. It was a Saturday night and I was alone again. I had a lot of bills to pay, a fiancé with no job, a full day of work the next day. On top of this, my great-grandmother had just passed away. The next day I would have the difficult experience of styling the hair of the grandmother I had loved, as well as my first experience doing the challenging job of styling hair at a mortuary. I knew I had to get it together and not give up.

As I sat there and looked in the mirror, I hated myself. I hated my freckles, my skin was so fair, and my hair was a cross between auburn and sun-bleached red. Although I made everyone else happy and beautiful all day long at the salon, I was miserable. How could I keep putting on this show? I wished I could be tanned like the other girls at the lake. I wished I was a blonde, or, better yet, a brunette with that dark skin to match my dark eyes. All of my other siblings were blonde and beautiful. I felt like the ugly duckling of the bunch. My self esteem was as low as a girl's could get.

I wanted to call the pastor to cancel my Sunday school class for the next morning, because I questioned my being qualified to teach it. There were only about twelve people left in that little Baptist Church, and the only children left in Sunday school were the ones I picked up and brought, and that included my little brothers and sisters and their three or four friends. Why did I get myself so involved in every-thing? Why did I think I always had to be Superwoman? I wanted to quit every good thing that had ever happened to me, but I couldn't think of any good things.

I cried for what seemed like hours. I remembered that there was a bottle of whiskey in the trunk of my car, left by a friend of my boyfriend. I wondered what it would be like to just drink the whole thing and not care, just like most kids my age, and then I reached for the button to pop the trunk.

In my rear view mirror I noticed an old rusted-out Volare with two guys in it, and it appeared that someone was approaching my car. I was half scared wondering if it was one of my fiancé's friends coming to tell me who he was out with, but it was nobody I recognized at first. Looking out the window all I could see was a cut off shirt, a fine set of abs, and a crutch. Oh great, I thought, a guy with a broken leg who needs a ride. He leaned down to look in my window. I dried my tears in a hurry and saw that his friend with the unimpressive car drove off. They both laughed as if they had been enjoying the party down the street. His hair was long. He had that Keith Urban look going on way before it was in style, and he had the most beautiful blue eyes I had ever seen. I was too immersed in my own fears to notice that this was Dave, the very guy who had called me for a haircut that afternoon. He asked me for a ride. I told him I was a little scared for anyone to see him in my vehicle, but he opened the door any way and suggested that we take the back country roads. What a novel idea I thought. It was bad enough that we might be seen in town, let alone out on the country roads.

I forgot all about popping the trunk to get the bottle of whiskey as I turned my attention to getting the heck out of the parking lot and getting him delivered to where he wanted to go and out of my car as soon as possible. He looked over at me and smiled as he said, "You look nice tonight, and you smell good, too." I thanked him as I tried to hide the goose bumps on my legs and arms. I felt a little numb as I drove him to his friend's house. When we arrived, he beat on the door, but his friend and his rusted-out car were not there. I felt like I was in a game of cat and mouse, and I really wanted to just help him find his friend. I didn't want to get caught with him in my vehicle.

There are things that happen in our life that can change it in a moment. Some that we take advantage of, some that we miss, but there are always instances that can turn our lives around. I had no idea that this night would be the night that forever changed my life.

Sometimes when we ask God for things, we have to be careful. Not only do we have to be careful, but we have to listen to what He tells us, whether we like the answer or not. God has a plan for all of us in our lives. It is well thought out before we are even born. Although we can make choices at crossroads and that may determine the outcome, we are His children and He loves us like we love our own. He only wants happiness for all of us, but sometimes we are just hard to teach. I was always a little bit stubborn, but this time I thought I just might give in.

We then drove around in the darkness until 3:30AM until I was tired. He didn't talk much, which was no problem for me. I felt like talking and I didn't take breaths often, so he didn't have to worry about silence. He asked me a lot of questions, and for the first time in a very long time, I felt like someone cared. It had been a long time since I had someone compliment me. In fact, it had probably been since I was twelve years old when this same guy, Dave Pitcock, had sent me a rose and taken me to the movie. He was always a really nice guy, but not a person whose life I had followed through high school. I guess since that summer when we were twelve, everything had changed drastically, and we had a lot of catching up to do.

He couldn't believe it when I told him I was going to do my great-grandma's hair at the mortuary in four hours. The thought of that just freaked him out. He asked me all about what I did, and I told him. Part of me wondered what it would be like to just run free like he had with his career, and not worry about showing up at the salon, the dance school, and all of my other weekly meetings and commitments. I couldn't imagine doing what he did either—riding bulls professionally and traveling around with a car load of cowboys. It was fun listening to his stories. I was definitely entertained.

Soon the sun would be coming up. We stopped at the house where his mother now lived. It wasn't the house he grew up in, nor was my mom living in the house where he used to come to visit me. A lot had changed in ten years. We reminisced about his coming over to jump on my trampoline. He also reminded me that his friend Wetig would hold my baby brother for me so that he could kiss me goodbye before he ran home. Back then Dave had to try to beat it home before the street lights came on. He used to fear his dad would be there waiting if he was late. I would worry that my mom and dad might come home early, although they usually never got home from work until the wee hours of the morning.

When we were children Dave's mom and dad ran a western wear store, and my parents owned several businesses, including a food distribution company that kept both of them on the road in semi-trucks at least five days a week. I didn't mind taking care of the kids and putting them to bed. I loved my little brothers and sisters and dreamed of some day having my own, even though my mom and I butted heads so much I used to threaten that I would never have any kids.

In seventh grade life is just a fantasy. I believe that it is during those years that we are really influenced to become the person we will later be. It seemed like decades since we were both just kids at the movies with families that were picture-perfect to all of the other kids. I tried not to cry as Dave and I talked about our parents. It was all so fresh. Both of our parents had since divorced and, oddly enough, both of our dads made the decision to leave during our senior years of high school. We compared the survival stories of our moms, who were both single, trying to put the pieces together for us and the younger ones. Dave's mom was out of town that summer night in August. There was nobody home but the two of us and I was a little scared to be there at first. My trust in men was not very strong, but I didn't want to leave.

Dave talked to me like he was my best friend, and a few times he stopped talking and just looked at me like he was looking into some crystal ball. I didn't know how to explain this feeling, but I didn't want it to go away. We read the Pro-Rodeo Sports News until about 4:00AM I was somewhat intrigued that he had just had a major surgery and had been told he might never walk again. Yet he said he was so addicted to the adrenaline rush he couldn't wait to enter in another rodeo. There was a rodeo the next night in Abilene, Kansas. He planned to go there and then to see a friend on the Kansas State Campus after the rodeo. It sounded like a lot of fun to be somebody who didn't have a job, since I didn't often take off of work and go out.

The sun was coming up as he walked me back to my car. He walked close to me and opened my door. Although I had been out all night and in the presence of a male, I was innocent, and I knew it. Well, almost innocent. As he closed the door, he whispered to me, "I usually don't kiss a girl on the first date." Then he kissed me and walked away as if I might never see him again, but then, again, I might.

2

Was He an Angel Dressed As a Bull Rider?

I COULD HARDLY GET MY MIND OFF OF THIS GUY, but I freshened up my lipstick and brushed my hair. I decided to ask my sister, Lori, to come with me to the mortuary. I was a wreck, full of anxiety and conflict, not to mention that I had gone without sleep, and I had family coming to town for a funeral. I've always been teased that I talk a lot. I wondered if during that night in August of 1992 Dave Pitcock wished I would stop talking and leave, or whether it was as magical for him as for me. I had left his house only a few hours ago, and I couldn't wait to be in his presence again. I didn't understand why I wanted to go back to see him so badly. After all, I was engaged to be married to a man I had dated for ten years and had my own home and an established business. All of a sudden it was like I was crazy in love and nothing else mattered. But how could I be in love with someone after the first night we talked?

I had to tell someone what had happened. Nobody was home at my house, so I drove to my mother's. I told the little ones Lori and I would bring them back donuts. Lori always rode with my dad on his morning route with the milk truck, and she just assumed that everyone loved chocolate milk as much as she did. I told her we were going on a donut run, but not for the reason she thought. I didn't know if Dave and his brother loved chocolate milk and donuts, but I wanted to use her as an excuse to go back to Dave's house. My sister was like my rock. I could depend on her to stand by me through thick and thin. I confessed to her about my prayers, my fears, and that I had just sat up all night talking to this new friend, and I had never felt this way in all of my life. She gave me a high five and congratulated me for landing what would be most girls' dream come true.

It was 9:00AM and it was only two hours since I'd seen Dave. And here I was with Lori beating on the Pitcock boys' door. Lori, without a shy bone in her body, ran in the front door and greeted Dave's little brother, her friend Scott, with chocolate donuts and chocolate milk. Suddenly I was feeling so secure, and I felt different when I looked at myself in the mirror. But I was falling in love with this busted-up rodeo cowboy who didn't even have a job. Heck, I didn't even know if he had a car. Besides the rusted-out Volare in the front yard there was a small little silver Fiero with a thirty-day tag that said "Lookin' for 8" on the front tag. He laughed hysterically when I asked him if he played pool. My sister called me an airhead as she explained that the "8" was for staying on a bull for an eight seconds for a qualified ride. I didn't know a lot about rodeo, but I was interested in learning anything that had to do with him and his passion. He invited me to go along to Abilene to the rodeo, and I couldn't say no.

Twenty-four hours later we were on the way to the rodeo. I poured myself into a western pair of jeans, dug out my white ropers and spent more time in the bathroom than I had since my first day of high school. I had a real date. This time it was one with a friend, and in the back of my mind I knew it was probably too good to be true. I thought, "How long could this last?" as we drove down I-70 to the Abilene exit. "What will happen when I get home? How will I ever get myself out of this mess?" I had to chuckle as I looked down at the engagement ring I bought for myself, and the wedding I was planning on my own. A fantasy wedding. I had spent years with one guy while praying and hoping he would love me back. That was the first night I had ever entertained the thought of getting out of that mess. Is this what it would be like to be happy?

Def Leppard, an 80's rock band, was playing on the radio. Dave could only drive with one leg and there was a crutch propped up by the driver's side door. He didn't say a lot, but he was singing the song, "Have you ever needed someone so bad?" I wanted to answer him, but I felt like a total geek. Using one leg on the gas and the same leg for the clutch he grabbed my hand and kissed me. At that time I made a decision I was never going back to my old life. I wanted to spend the rest of my life like this, and I hoped he would feel the same way. I didn't want to get my hopes up, and with my low self-esteem I was far from believing I was good enough for him.

We watched the rodeo that night, and then went to the Kansas State Campus where his friend lived. That night I was getting a little worried about my family wondering where I was. I called home to and told them to let people know I was with a friend, who was staying with her grandmother who was dying of cancer. How horrible of me to have to lie. The worst part of my story was that they were all going to pray for her.

Dave laughed at the fact that he didn't have a dime. He hadn't been able to work or ride for a month and was just recently able to get off the couch. Fourth of July had been a near death experience for Dave in Crawford, Nebraska. He had a bull-riding accident that landed him in the Scotts Bluff Hospital for several days. He was told several surgeries later he might not be able to walk again. His leg was about the size of a chicken leg, but the rest of him, I must admit, I thought was looking pretty good. At first I thought it was the Wrangler jeans or maybe it was the cowboy hat. I didn't know what it was for sure, but I was definitely falling hard.

We ended up in Great Bend, Kansas in a single-wide trailer with Chris LeDoux blaring rodeo stories to what Dave called music. His brother, Scott, worked in Great Bend and had just gotten a week's worth of pay, and Dave and his brother were headed to New Mexico to see Billy the Kid's grave. Scott was always a little bit of an outlaw himself and he was excited about the trip. I knew that it was a guy thing, and I would have to go back to reality. Besides, I probably had tons of messages, many appointments at the salon, and a load of little girls to teach at Sunday school that week. There was no such thing as a cell phone then. I thought about going to a pay phone to call home to tell them I wouldn't be home that night, but the thought didn't last long. I said good-bye to Dave and Scott, and I had to laugh at this cowboy, his rock-star brother, and their plans to go on vacation with their $300. 00.

When I got home that night I sat alone for several hours. I wanted to run, but I didn't know where to go. I couldn't tell my mother, because she would think I was crazy. My sister, her boyfriend, and the guy who I had been engaged to were in the harvest fields. I knew it would be an all-night deal for them, swathing the alfalfa fields. So I sat down with a pen and paper and I wrote a letter that I was planning to leave for a while. I didn't know where to tell them I was going but I told them that I just had to leave. Most young girls would go to their father, but mine had been gone for a long time. My dad was in

South Dakota where he had been hiding from my mom and family for about four years. That Christmas we had finally located him, and there were a lot of questions in my mind and a lot of insecurities. Was it that bad? Was I not someone he loved enough to stick around? Would he even care if I called him crying and said, "Daddy, I'm scared and I don't know what to do?"

I remembered back to the last night he was home. He left my senior year in 1989, the night of my prom. It was just two weeks after I learned for the first time that he wanted a separation. My mom and dad never fought and there had been no signs of problems in the marriage that would lead to a divorce.

That starry night in May I was dressed in my floor length prom dress as a queen candidate at Russell High School. The other girls were all much prettier than me; I really didn't know how I was nominated and I was so nervous. As we posed for family pictures by the oak tree in the driveway, I told my little sister Traci to pray for me. She was my pride and joy, and she was only four years old.

Just then the sheriff drove into our driveway and handed my mom some papers. I had no idea what they were about, but mom seemed uneasy as we posed for pictures with my dad's mom. I didn't understand why my mom was so emotional when I told Traci to let Daddy hold her in the pictures. After taking the family photos I headed to the crowning, but being prom queen was the last thing on my mind that evening after I realized the seriousness of my parents' problems

Two weeks after those papers were served, Dad fled with a woman from our home town. We had no idea where he went for the next four years. It was hard on me, my mom, and most of all, those little ones who wouldn't know their daddy.

In 1992 those years seemed long ago to me and I was now a young woman. I felt like I deserved an explanation for his leaving us. Although I butted heads with my dad growing up and he was a strong disciplinarian, I just longed to run to someone far away. I wanted to be loved and I wanted someone that would listen. I knew that the friends and family around me in this small town would all think I was crazy.

My dad was usually pretty honest with me and supported me as far as decisions I made in my high school years. He always encouraged me to work hard and strive for my goals and dreams, but he had left me. I don't know why I thought he would listen to me. I hated him at the time for what he had done, but deep-down I loved him because he was my dad. I knew that going to see him was a good excuse to leave and I made the decision to find him. I had $20.00 left from hair cuts from the previous Saturday, but that was it, after running around with my new cowboy friend all week. All I had was a tank of gas, a change of clothes, and my blow dryer. I put the top down on the convertible, and I drove. For the first time in so long I felt free—just running with the wind. I was running but I didn't get far.

Dave had helped me plan the trip to see my dad. Trusting Dave, I never checked my own map. I simply took his directions he said would get me to my dad's home in South Dakota, and I just drove! Dave had given me a number to call him if I needed him. I didn't get far before I stopped at the first pay phone I found. He met me at a convenience store where I phoned him. He wished me well on the rest of my journey and I wished him well on his.

I never was very good at geography. I just passed it to get through school so I could graduate and go to work. It never dawned on me that it was strange that the map Dave marked to help me to get to South Dakota had Kansas City marked as half-way there.

When I called my dad from a phone in Kansas City, Missouri, he informed me that Kansas City was way out of the way to come to his house in South Dakota. I realized that Dave must have planned to meet me all along. When I then called Dave he said they were coming to join me. I never meant to crash Dave and Scott's trip to Mexico, but I caused them to change their route. I then ran off with them to Branson, Missouri with $320 between us.

Dave was used to traveling and he didn't have a lot of worries. We just made plans from one day to the next how we would eat and where we would stay. It was the greatest week of my life. The top of my convertible broke, and Scott had a hard time listening to his 3-foot jam box in the wind with his long hair tangling around the speakers. My fair skin was freckling to the point I thought it would be totally brown, but I couldn't get that lucky. The hot summer wind was beating us to death, but the top of the convertible was jammed and we couldn't close it. Other than that, we didn't have a care in the world! We just drove and drove until the sun went down that night, and then we looked for the cheapest hotel with some food and a shower. It was the summer of 1992, and God was answering every prayer I had asked for in His own time. He didn't tell me that there would be some setbacks, but He had given me a "Best Friend." "For every adversity, there is a gift."

One night Dave encouraged me to call my dad to tell him where I was just to get it off my chest. I told my dad the truth and he knew that I was scared. I couldn't believe I was calling him after my mother and I had suffered through so much with the kids and his leaving. I didn't like him for what he had done, but Dave said he understood completely. He was still my dad. Everyone else in my family questioned my sanity, but my dad just listened.

That night Dave pulled out a book called *Psycho-Cybernetics: A New Way to Get More Living Out of Life* by Maxwell Maltz. I thought it was for crazy people or something. I might have qualified, but Dave taught me a lot that night. He told me I had a lot of baggage, a lot of fears, and a very low self-esteem. Even though I had a booming business, a fancy little sports car, and a nice home, I was not happy. And I feared that when I went home to my boyfriend I might just get killed. But what would happen to my business, my bills, my relationship, my little brothers and sisters if I didn't return? How would my mom manage working at the factory, cleaning houses, and running the RV Park? I had helped her so much, and we worked together to always survive no matter what had happened.

When we were standing in the parking lot in Kansas City there was just enough light from the street lights to see Dave's eyes. I trusted this guy, and I listened to him even though I didn't want to hear what he was saying at that time in my life. I wondered about him after listening to the music he was playing at the trailer park where I visited him, but this book thing was even weirder. What kind of a guy reads *Psycho-Cybernetics* and listens to Chris LeDoux's music? He was a lot smarter than I knew at the time.

Dave put his finger on the trunk and drew two boxes on the dust of that red convertible. He told me this box is you and this box is your problems. The most important thing is that you never let your fears about your temporary situation become bigger than you are. You need to put them all in this box and see yourself bigger than that. "Barb, you are bigger than that," he promised me.

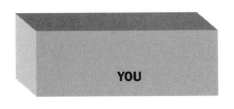

It was a crazy two weeks when I returned home from our trip. So many things happened, but looking back now I can laugh. One thing Dave taught me was not to be too hard on ourselves then, because we would be laughing later. At the time it was hard to believe. We didn't have much of a choice except to run away because the small town we both lived in was buzzing like a bunch of bees with stories, opinions, and a lot of free advice. Sometimes the people you love the most give you their advice and you trust them more than you trust yourself. Not this time. I knew what happiness felt like for the first time in my life, and I even think I was falling in love. Everyone told me I was crazy.

My answering machine was full of people wanting salon services, and I was so busy that my mother made a trip to the supply warehouse to keep me stocked for the busy week ahead. She questioned whether I was having a nervous breakdown, and by then my relationship with my fiancé was definitely on the rocks. My brothers and sisters were so attached to my previous life that they were having a hard time supporting my break-up, because change is hard no matter what kind of change it is. People always tend to stay in their comfort zones and not risk anything that might rock the boat. This time I didn't care if the boat rocked, tipped, or sunk! It was going to be worth it for me to try it. My head was saying, "You must be crazy," but my heart was saying, "Crazy in love!"

A few weeks later I ran away with Dave Pitcock to Cody, Wyoming, 950 miles from my home. We didn't have jobs or a plan. The first night we were in Cody we went to a cheap hotel on South Fork Road, the gateway to Yellowstone National Park. The only reason we went there was because we knew about a nightly rodeo near the mountains that his grandmother and uncle had talked about. We decided to rent a house and look for jobs, all in the same weekend. You never know why things happen the way they do, but looking back today I know the lessons that we learned. It was called survival.

The first week we had a little bit of cash from Dave's final pay check from the utility company he worked for in Kansas. The next week would be my first week working at a salon on the famous tourist Main Street. The only problem with the famous Main Street in Cody, Wyoming is that it shuts down from October until about April, and we moved there on Halloween. My whole first two weeks' commission after waiting for appointments from nine to five every day except Sunday was seventy-four dollars. I used to make that in one morning.

Many times I was tempted to go back to what was so easy for me, but I never questioned that I needed to stay there with Dave. He tried to find a job for two solid months, and the only thing he could find was refilling the ice skating rink at night. At times the winds were cold enough to freeze the water as fast as he could shoot it out of the fire hydrant. The job paid seven dollars an hour, and that was a lot to us. I remember standing there with him watching the water freeze on his beard. He grew the beard only to keep warm in those cold mountains of Wyoming.

Our little cabin was a cozy little place, so cozy that the ice would freeze on the inside of the shower as you washed. I would put several layers of clothes on at night and pull every blanket off the beds to snuggle up next to the wood-burning stove. We didn't dare let the flame die in the stove or it would be instantly cold throughout the entire house. Dave put the battery from the car inside next to the fire at night to keep it from freezing up completely, and we would plug in the block to warm the engine enough to start. It was cold, but it was worth it to be together so far away from home and to be able to think clearly about what it was we both wanted.

Since we had both just ended long-term relationships, there were days when Dave and I struggled with our emotions. We talked a lot about our fears, our dreams, and the things that we couldn't keep hidden in the closet. When the weather was nice Dave would play his harmonica on the back porch and sit out in the little tool shed for hours at night. I always worried that he didn't want to be there with me. I was so insecure that even a phone call from a friend back home would make me wonder if he had romantic feelings for her, or if he was wishing he was back there. I couldn't stand the thought of losing him.

Our moms would call and check on us. Dave's uncle sent $100.00 for Christmas. To survive financially we sold off everything back home, including my horse I had since my thirteenth birthday. We were barely able to pay our bills, and we were too proud to ask for help from our parents. I remember sitting in church and watching Dave give half of our money as I trembled in fear that we would starve to death without it. He always told me to go on faith.

I will never forget the lecture Dave gave me on getting by. He asked me if I had ever gone without or if I always managed to get by. I never thought of it that way, but he said God always provides us with what we need. We need to worry less because it is a waste of time. Some days I felt like I was living with a freak. His outlook on things was so different from what I was used to. He said that we should just go to the courthouse and get married so we weren't living in sin, but I wanted no part of that. I was still dreaming of that big wedding that every girl dreams of. I had waited my whole life to walk down that aisle with someone who loved me. I didn't want to do it at a courthouse.

Dave read the Bible for hours every day looking for all the answers that he might never find. "Why do things happen the way they do?" he would ask, and "Where is God when bad things are happening to good people?" I didn't question God. I just trusted that He was going to take care of me and that is all that kept me from the fears in my head at night. "How do you know?" he would ask. "How will we ever know if He is real, when He is coming, where He is, and what He wants us to do?" Dave was frustrated as he read the Bible cover to cover every day while I sat at the salon in this little ghost town waiting for my next $10.00 haircut from which I would make a fifty percent commission. Tips were my only hope, because paychecks were cut only once every two weeks. I never thought of myself as a flirt, but when that once a week rancher came in for his haircut, I was definitely working for that $2.00 tip!

I hated my job there. I didn't like to sit around, and I was surrounded by a bunch of girls who loved to gossip, lie, cheat, and drum up trouble. I stuck it out and I recruited some clients from our church, along with a neighbor, just so I could get some appointments on the book. Each night Dave would pick me up from work and educate me about what he had learned that day. Many times I thought he would become a preacher. He was so good; he even had me believing miracles were going to happen, and they were happening every day if I would just notice them.

The week when we lined up at the food pantry to get our shares was the most humbling thing I had ever done in my life, but we needed some food in the cupboards. There were a lot of people who were much worse off than we were. This was it! I was at the bottom of my barrel and we had to find a way to make some money.

Dave and I sat down one night dreaming of how we could survive. What did we like to do, what would we be good at? He started making some crafts out of scrap wood and I painted the wood he cut out. It was fun and it gave him something new to do in his favorite place, the tool shed.

We went to the bank to see if we could borrow some money, and we made plans to open a Christian book store so we could share our faith with others through good books. Dave was on a mission to influence other people with his strong beliefs and convictions. I thought it would be a lot of fun and I dreamed of decorating our store front. We called home to tell our family, and boy did they think we had totally lost our minds. My old circle of friends didn't call me much, and they all laughed at my transformation from the little entrepreneur in the red convertible to the girl who lost it all when she ran away from home.

It was tough to go back to Russell and visit, but we did go for Christmas. It was especially tough to pull into my mom's driveway and see that my ex-boyfriend hadn't even gotten his own place. Once I moved, he just moved in with my family. I couldn't even stay at my own mom's house; we both had to go to Dave's mom's house for the night. It really hurt, but I didn't give in to opinions. The more they told me I was crazy, the more stubborn I became. My mom was pretty supportive, but the sister I was so close to was taking the side of the very guy she watched hurt me so badly.

Lori and I didn't talk for about a year. I wrote letters to Traci, Mark, and Jeremy telling them that I loved them and missed them, but had to be away right now. My youngest sister still has the letters I sent. It is so important to tell people that you love them and express your true feelings, because they cannot know your mind. I would write daily in journals and send letters to those I missed. I didn't know why I was so far away from home, but I knew that this was my new life.

That week after Christmas I packed all of my belongings in the rag top, since we were planning to head back to Cody. I noticed a wrecker in my mother's driveway and my little red convertible was being winched onto the trailer. I cried, but I knew it was coming. There was no way we could afford this little car. I guess I just didn't know they would take it so soon. I was only two payments behind, and I kept thinking if the bank would approve the loan for our book store, I could catch up on all my past payments. I was devastated when they hauled it out of my mother's driveway but Dave didn't get too rattled. He was determined to get us back to the mountains, and we were anxious to go back to our safe little world so far away from where we grew up. The wrecker took the car right down Main Street to make it clear to all of my friends that it was repossessed, but that didn't slow us down. We borrowed my mother's old Cougar and we set back out on the highway for what we now called home. Although I hated to leave my friends and family, going home wasn't the same this time. They didn't all agree with my new plans and some of them were a little bit cold.

The lesson I learned was that you have to get away from your old environment to truly do what it takes to become the person you are supposed to be. It's not that you have to move a thousand miles away, but you must leave home and get out of that rut in order to make decisions in your life. I had never done this before. It was so hard, but it was so good.

My mother kissed me and hugged me goodbye in a way she had never done before as we headed out on the trip back west. Mom was never a really affectionate person; tough love was always the way it was at our house. She was a hard worker with calloused hands, and the signs of manual labor were in her face and her build. She could work circles around most men. She had learned that from her own mother, my grandma who raised me as a child while my mom and dad worked so many hours. I didn't know what my mother was thinking, but she loved David Pitcock. She said it was his blue eyes that won her over, but I think she admired the way he was so caring and humble about himself. He didn't say much, but he was sincere, and that is what I loved so much about him.

It was January, and we were planning a June wedding. I was so excited to decorate the church and have a big wedding, but when it got right down to it, being married to my best friend was so much more important than having the big show. We planned a conservative wedding, instead of spending money that we didn't have to buy stuff to impress all of my friends and family. We opted for a log cabin church in the country about forty-five minutes from Russell and planned to invite a couple hundred of our friends and family. As I planned this day, I dreamed of going to Kansas again to visit the people I missed so badly.

The book *Psycho-Cybernetics* did more for me than Dave ever imagined. It helped me understand the power of my subconscious mind and how to focus on the things I wanted to happen in my life, rather than worry about the things I feared might happen. Each day I dreamed of moving back home and starting our family. I could just imagine hugging my little brothers and sisters and having them stay over with us on the weekends. I missed them all so much and I couldn't imagine being so far from everyone for much longer. I kept reading that book and remembering when he gave it to me on that first date. I put the laws into practice, and before I knew it Dave received a call from his former boss back in Kansas. He was offered an amazing position with the fiber-optic phone line company and they even offered to come and move us.

The U-haul was backed up to our little Wyoming cabin as we were packing to move back home, and a gorgeous deer came walking across the front lawn and made his way up the mountain behind our home. It was beautiful there and I knew Dave would miss it. I felt so sad to make him move back to Kansas, but no matter where you go and how beautiful it is, true happiness comes when you are filled with love for those who are around you. I loved him with all my heart but I ached every day for my family.

As we pulled into the State of Kansas, we imagined the wheat fields blowing. Yes, it was flat and what many would call ugly, but to me it was the most beautiful land I had seen in months. I couldn't wait to watch the sunset over the plains. There would be deer and antelope in Kansas, too. There just wouldn't be any mountains to climb.

Our little house in Great Bend, Kansas was small, and our rent was just two hundred dollars a month. I was excited to return home. Dave didn't say much except he was glad that I was happy.

3

Like Two Sparrows
in a Hurricane

IF YOU HAD TOLD ME that I would walk down the aisle and marry David Pitcock just twelve months prior to the day I did, I would have put my index finger to your temple and would have drawn a few small circles. It was almost like living in a cloud or some dream world to be so happy and so full of hope, when just months prior to that I was so desperate for love and so empty inside.

April 10, 1993, was a windy day in Kansas, and Dave and I joked that we were two sparrows in a hurricane. There was a song out that mentioned just that:

Two sparrows in a hurricane, trying to find their way ...
with a head full of dreams and faith that could move anything.
They've heard it's all uphill, all they know is how they feel.
The world says they'll never make it, love says they will.
Tanya Tucker ... She didn't know when she sang the song just how uphill it would be!

I know it was a tough day for our moms who saw both of our fathers with their new partners. Knowing that their hearts were breaking, Dave and I tried to make the ceremony something that was special. Then we opted for a short and sweet reception instead of the wedding dance and reception I had always dreamed of. Although I always dreamed of the dance I would have with my father, or having my mother there at the head table, it seemed a lot more appropriate to simply cut the cake and send the crowd on their way. Dave and I

21

were so in love. It really didn't matter to us how impressive the ceremony was because we knew the most important part of the day was that we were united as one, and we would start our own family soon. We took a quick honeymoon to Branson, Missouri with the $500.00 from wedding gifts and the extra money we had managed to save. We drove through Springfield, stopping off at the Bass Pro Shop and then headed to Silver Dollar City. With the spontaneous personality that Dave had, we had no plan—just a map to get us to the next place we chose. Since we didn't have any reservations at all, it wasn't until we got to Silver Dollar City and we were the only ones in the parking lot, that we realized the park did not open for two more weeks. We laughed and took pictures of ourselves in front of the sign with the arrows pointing to the parks and the chain hanging across the gate that read "Park closed for the season."

We played putt-putt golf and ordered pizza to our little economy hotel room and talked about our future. It is amazing how newly married couples can dream and how big their vision is when they first start out. We drove all the way back to Kansas the next day, stopping off to buy some hunting and fishing supplies at Bass Pro Shop. I gazed and dreamed at every ranch we passed and pointed out every house with pillars on it. Dave's dream was to be a professional bull-riding champion and mine was to fill a house full of kids and be a good wife. He dreamed of a double-wide trailer, and I was always trying to figure out how to top it off with a circle drive, a fountain, and some big white pillars. We were opposites in so many ways, but boy the attraction was there. We passed the Precious Moments Museum and didn't even stop off at any site-seeing attractions. We just made our way back to Great Bend, that was now our home, counting the few dollars we had left. Dave had a few days of vacation left before he had to return to the construction crew and go on the road for the week.

Monday through Friday Dave was a foreman for a fiber optic cable company that plowed phone lines. It was just a short drive to see our family in Russell. I usually went back to visit during the week to see my brothers and sisters. I was cutting hair just two days a week in Great Bend so I could make some extra money. I was on booth-rent, which was so different from when I had my own salon. I missed being my own boss, and I couldn't wait to re-open my own salon. I hadn't had a boss since I was waiting tables at the age of fourteen. It went totally against the grain and what I had been taught while growing up.

Dave wanted me to be home with our children while he worked. I couldn't wait to have babies, and we were expecting our first child in October. On September 7 I woke up and complained to Dave that my back was killing me. I was really good about walking every day and watching what I ate so my baby would be healthy. I kissed Dave goodbye and told him that in just one more month, I wouldn't have to complain about how uncomfortable I was. We would be parents soon!

At about 11AM the pain became severe. I called my mom, crying, and my sister Lori, drove to Great Bend from Russell. She and I had not been very close for many months since I went out west. It meant a lot to me that she came, but it was a strange feeling. I was crying when she got there. I called Dave's boss's wife, because I was so scared I knew I needed someone to pray with me. She was a saint in my eyes, a true prayer-warrior.

I remembered months ago when I was at my mom's house. I walked with a girl in the evenings who was expecting a baby about the same time mine was due. She delivered a healthy baby. However, she died several hours later of a rare disease called Toxemia. The fear of being really sick took over my mind for several days. I tried not to worry every day that I would get this rare disease. Pat, the company owner's wife, prayed with me. She assured me that I was in good hands and that God would take care of me and my baby. I had no idea back then about the power of the mind, but it is very clear to me today that "You become what you think about." Pat laid her hands on my tummy, prayed that the pain would go away, and suggested that we go see my doctor. I was a ballet teacher, and my biggest concern was that I could soon be back to teaching little kids. I didn't want to have a bunch of stitches or any problems. All along my doctor had assured me how healthy I was, that I would have a speedy recovery after delivery, and that the baby would be fine.

As I entered the doctor's office, my petite Filipino doctor was happy as usual, and she asked me to give her a urine sample. Moments later, I heard her on the phone calling a Wichita hospital and ordering a Life Watch helicopter to get me into the emergency room as soon as I arrived. What was going on? She stayed calm as she assured me I would be fine, but the look in my sister's eyes said something was definitely wrong. My doctor just said we needed to deliver the baby early.

We headed to the local hospital where I was Life Watched to Wichita. I remember that the drive from the doctor's office in the

Suburban was extremely painful, and Pat prayed the whole way while my sister sat in the back with a confused look on her face. I know Lori was scared enough to pray, but was reluctant to do so since several of our friends thought we were in some kind of a cult because of the way our church did praise, worship, and prayer. It was a spirit-filled church with a full band and a circle of friends that were closer than most families. Thank goodness I had this connection, or I do not know where I would be today.

Because Dave had never been able to take days off from work to go to the doctor's visits with me, my doctor had never met him. In spite of all the commotion at the hospital my little doctor, who stood all of 4.5 feet, let out a squeal next to my bed when Dave arrived. Dave left the construction site to go home to quickly shower. When he walked in wearing his black cowboy hat and brightly colored Garth Brooks western shirt, the doctor made a point to tell me my husband was good looking!

I don't know how fast my family drove to Wichita, Kansas to their large medical center, but the three-hour drive definitely did not take them three hours. Dave called his mom at the local Pizza Hut where she was having lunch, and told her to get my mother and come quickly. They arrived shortly after we did!

I was in ICU for a couple of days as they tried to regulate my blood pressure. I didn't know what was going on. They just told me to stay lying on my left side and keep my right arm above my head. I had needles and wires connected to toes and fingers. My chest even had sticky band aids holding wires to monitors.

After we all spent sleepless nights with my family standing by my bedside, they tried to induce labor, not knowing if it was safe to do this when my blood pressure was so high. I didn't realize my life was in danger until a nurse came in to take my blood. I remember well when she went to take blood from a vein in my right hand. The blood showered her and went all over the room. That's when she mentioned my blood was thinned, and it was just part of the disease. What disease? I had a disease? I don't think she knew it was a secret to me when everyone else in my family knew. It turned out that I had developed Toxemia HELLP Syndrome, the rare disease that had taken the life of my friend just months ago. I was shocked, thinking, "But this is such a rare disease." I was told that only one in every 100,000 women actually get it. There seemed no chance that I could get this. My doctor had assured me I was so healthy.

Now I understood the faces of my family looking in the glass window with tears in their eyes. No wonder my sister had driven so fast, and no wonder everyone was praying. Dave assured me he was not scared. He told me everything would be just fine. I didn't know until later that he was told the baby would be fine; it was the mommy they were worried about.

On the morning of September 10 they did an emergency C-section, not wanting to wait any longer since both my liver and kidneys had shut down. I swelled up like a big blimp, with almost no nose or chin because I was so puffy. I couldn't hear a thing. My ear drums had burst from the pressure and were draining.

When I opened my eyes, I could see tears streaming down Dave's face. I heard her crying as Dave laid our new daughter under my chest and said, "It's a girl!" She was beautiful! She had dark hair, dark eyes, and was just less than five pounds of nothing but long fingers, long toes, and a handful of blanket. I just laid there and prayed that everything would be fine, and I would be healthy again. Brooklyn Nicole was our little miracle baby. Dave's brother had long hair down his back and tattoos all down his arm, but my little angel dressed in pink even made him turn to mush. My baby was beautiful and I was a mom. I just wanted to be well.

It was hard for me to learn to breast feed because I couldn't hear a thing. Dave was very supportive as he took care of Brooklyn while I was wired up like a piece of electronic equipment. My blood pressure began to rise, and it was 240 over 120 when they took all of the family away from me. Even three days later they only allowed me to have ice chips and no liquid. Why was this happening? I was getting scared and I didn't want to be away from my baby and my husband. Dave was so faithful and attentive. He just kept caressing my hand between the needles, telling me it will all be okay. I felt so helpless and alone.

Dave had never even taken care of a younger sibling, since his brother was just a few years younger than he was. His brother Scott, and my sister Lori, were the same age. It was I who had four younger brothers and sisters and had been such a little mother my whole life. I told him during the whole pregnancy not to worry about learning all of this. I'll teach you everything. Now, I was laying in a bed in ICU as he learned to change her diaper, take her temperature, hold her up to me to feed her, and even rock her to sleep while I wished I could just get up and take care of her myself.

There were over twenty people in the waiting room outside of the ICU unit. I remember my doctors saying to them, "She cannot have this commotion right now. Even a phone ringing raises her blood pressure." Maybe my doctor didn't realize that it might have been because my dad was the one who called. It could have been the stress of that call that further increased the pressure.

It wasn't easy for Dave and me with both of our parents divorced, both moms alone, and fathers that had remarried. There was always an uncomfortable feeling when we were with our moms and the subject of our fathers came up. My mom was my rock, and I didn't understand why someone so special should have to survive such pain as a single mom and spend times like this without my father by her side. There are some questions for which you never find an answer, but there must be a reason.

About a dozen people from our church showed up at the hospital. Although my Grandma Schneider thought our church was a cult, they managed to get past her and the security to my bedside. Grandma Schneider was my dad's mom and she raised her four kids and three step-children in the Catholic Church. I don't know what religion I was as a child. My grandma on my mom's side baptized me Baptist and I went there every Sunday. Once she passed away I would occasionally go with Grandma Schneider to the Catholic Church. I always believed in God, but since Dave and I had been married, I had grown much closer to Him. The Protestant Church we attended focused more on the relationship with Him than the particular religion. Grandma was praying with her beads, and the people in my room were praying with their hands on me or in the air. Who knows who is right and who is wrong, but I will tell you what happened in that room. Within twenty minutes of them praying over me, my blood pressure was normalized. I was put in a regular room with no roommate and had the hope of a drink if I could keep my blood pressure normal.

I was so thankful, and Dave was smiling from ear to ear as they unhooked all of the wires. I finally got to see all of my family in the hallway in route to my room. My blood pressure did go back up with activity, so they kept me on my side and limited my visitors. Regardless of what the monitors said and regardless of the team of seven doctors assigned to my medical case, none of them knew the power of my God. It was a miracle! It was the second miracle I had experienced in a matter of one year. God was so real to me. I wanted to spend every day of my life telling everyone what He had done in my life. It didn't take me long to realize that nobody else was as excited about that story as I was, and many of them thought I was a freak. I was on a roll, a born-again Christian thinking I was going to save the world!

Soon after I recovered I took my entire family of brothers, sisters, and mom to the front of a Billy Graham Revival in Great Bend. Dave and I made sure that they all went to the front. I didn't want anyone to go without this gift of His love in their life. After taking them, I guess we thought everyone would understand our faith, but that was not the case. Some people thought we were crazy, and others just avoided us at all costs. My old circle of friends back home got a kick out of the fact that their old buddy had lost her mind, run off with a rodeo cowboy, and now we attended a church that they were all convinced was a cult!

The lesson I learned is that people don't deal well with change. People don't always understand. It is easier to condemn others for what they are doing, rather than researching the facts, because they aren't comfortable in their own situation. All things happen for a reason and being in Great Bend for that first year was important in my life. Dave and I had time away from all of our close friends and family to truly sprout our wings and fly our own way without any outside influences. It was a foundation that I would grow from for the rest of my life.

On September 12 we brought our little girl home to our rental house. I had decorated a nursery with a staple gun and blue wallpaper. I was so sure she was going to be a little boy that we would dress up in spurs and boots. Thank goodness everything wasn't all blue. There was a pink bow on one teddy bear in the border of the room and we accented it in pink. Our miracle, Brooklyn, cost a quarter of a million dollars by the time it was all said and done. Dave and I couldn't wait to be on our feet, and have our own health insurance and a steady income that was enough to support our growing family. We had a lot of dreams.

Dave was taking night classes at Barton County Community College on the evenings when his crew was in town. It was not so often that it made it hard to concentrate, but his mom had inspired him to finish his degree after all the years he had spent moving from college to college while he was riding bulls. Dave was a good bullrider. He rode eighty percent of the bulls he got on. The only problem was that he got hurt a lot.

We usually traveled to a rodeo each weekend. I would be so anxious to hear that diesel pickup pulling down the street to our little rental house. I missed him so much during the week when he was gone, and I worried about him in a hotel room with all of the other construction guys. Some of them were really nice guys, and I will just say he always had some interesting stories about others when he got home on Friday.

Dave's boss and his wife were great people. They invited us to the church where we were married, and they were incredibly strong in their faith. It was nice to be surrounded by people who truly cared about others, and Dave was very loyal to them as an employee. No matter how loyal he was, it was hard for me to think of him working for someone else the rest of our lives. I would tell him all of my ideas of businesses we could start and all the things we could do. He would look at me and smile as he sat up doing his home work for those college courses, trying to get the next good grade on some essay or test in some class that I had no idea how he would ever use in real life. But I was supportive of his education and even helped him write some of his papers, because writing was pretty easy for me. I remember one night in particular. We sat up until about 3AM writing an English story for his professor, whose husband was a pharmacist in a small town outside of Hays, Kansas. She drove back and forth to teach at Barton County, and if I could find her today, I would tell her, "Thank You." The grade she gave Dave on that paper changed our lives forever. At 3AM that morning Dave decided to go to sleep to get ready for another day on the construction crew, but he was excited to turn in his paper.

The story and dialogue were good and the English was perfect, because we proofread it over and over before he put it in the binder she had requested. Even the two dollar binder we put it in was a sacrifice back then, not to mention the time and effort. Dave didn't have class for several more days, but he was anxious to see what she would say about his paper. That night he came in, and the look on his face was not what I expected. As he threw his paper down on the table he said to me, "How could she do this?" She had given him an "F" on the paper we thought was so good. I remember him saying, "I can't do this. I hate this class. She could have at least given me a "D" for effort. An "F" would have been the same as if I turned nothing in!" He had tears in his eyes from the anger, and that night I told Dave, "Quit, just quit! And we will go and start our own business and make more in a day than she probably makes in a week!" Why would you let someone who is working for someone else control your destiny and tell you what you are worth? Now, having my own children, it would be hard for me to say those words, but boy was I mad that she had done this to my husband.

It was that day that we drove to our home town looking for a building to rent for a salon and a craft and furniture shop. I intended to cut hair, teach dance, and make some little craft things, and Dave would be the woodworker who would cut them out for me to paint. We were gonna' be rich! Boy this could work! We would just show that teacher how smart we were, in spite of her red pen on his paper. Within three months of that day we moved to Russell and opened "The Olde Tower," an abandoned old pizza place on the corner of Russell's two busiest streets. We had 6,000 square feet to grow in.

I took Brooklyn to work with me when I cut hair and I started to make some pretty good money on a daily basis. Dave and I had some pine furniture we had built and put in the shop for sale. He could make five quilt racks in one day and sell them for more than he would make in an entire week of working out of town. We were working smarter, instead of working harder. He took Brooklyn with him some times, and I would cut hair while he worked in the shop. She was three months old the day I pulled into the shop and held up the evidence of a positive pregnancy test. I was crying, fearful that I would have another near fatal pregnancy, and Dave was smiling ear to ear saying, "Cool, Brooky, you're going to have a little brother!" He was right, and that following November we were blessed with a healthy little boy we named Chance David, and the entire pregnancy and delivery was one hundred percent normal. They took Chance early to avoid any blood pressure issues since a C-section was mandatory for me. He was definitely healthy, weighing in at seven pounds nine ounces, even though he was a little early.

It was a little tougher to take two babies to work and cut hair all day, but now I was making several hundred dollars a day. So it wasn't too tough to pay a babysitter to help out. It felt like there was a ton of cash flow in that little business. We hired a helper to run the front desk of our shop so it made it easier for Dave and me to do income-producing activities. I had no idea at the time that she was tearing up sales receipts for purchases and putting them in the trash while she pocketed more per day than we were taking home. We continued to work hard day in and day out making ends meet, and sometimes I would wonder, "Where does all the money go?" It wasn't until we did an inventory of the sixty consigners in our gift store that we realized a lot was sold, but not much of it made it into our checking account.

At first I was very bitter and angry. After all, I was working as hard as I possibly could. I was a very trusting person and thought that most people were honest—and they are, but that doesn't mean that in business there aren't some lessons to be learned. This was just the beginning of our lessons.

Dave was constantly looking for the closest rodeo he could enter. As a supportive wife I didn't want to steal his dreams, yet I had fear. I can remember working all week to make a few hundred dollars, and then driving the miles to Dodge City to unload that double stroller behind the shoots, and pray as he strapped his hand onto a 2,000-pound bovine that wanted to kill him. He did pick up a check, although the money wasn't nearly as good then as it is today for professional bull-riding.

Dave was not doing it for the money. He didn't do anything for the money. To him money was just paper. He made that point very clear to me. I would fret about the lack of it and I would fret about the future. Dave would hand me a book like *Psycho-Cybernetics* or some self-help book, and I always wanted to remind him, "Hello, I am the mother of two babies. I do not have time to sit around and read!" Little did I know he was right. The more I would fret, the more challenges I had. He used to tell me I was a worrier. I guess I was, but that seemed the normal thing to be as our bills piled up. He was always looking, always thinking, and always open to a new and better way. He had a strong faith that made me feel like he should have been a preacher, instead of a bull-rider. Sometimes it was his faith that got me through the sleepless nights when the bills and the debts were high, and the funds were low, but we were determined to dig out of it.

I took those babies to day care at seven AM and begin to cut hair and wait on people in the gift store. We had several tanning beds busy at the salon, and a young woman who did acrylic nails. I did not collect any rent from her, even though she made a pile of cash each day on her own. She helped me out in the salon, and some days she would pick up the kids for me at dark if I was still busy. If she hadn't cleaned a little for me, I don't know how I would have kept going. I didn't confront her about the money. My husband would tell me that if people don't offer, then they must need money more than we did, and we should let them keep it. That would always stick in my mind, but I truly believed at that time that I needed it much more. Dave was always giving more than we had to give and always offering more than I wanted to offer, but he had me convinced that good things were in store for us.

I trusted Dave and although I had been the entrepreneur, he seemed to be pretty good at all he did, no matter what it was. We would enter a weekend craft show several hours from home and haul all of our hand-made furniture and country décor to some park and set up in the dark at 5AM for the weekend show. I have no idea how we unloaded trailers and sold things like we did with two small babies, but we did very well at most shows. Then again, sometimes the Kansas wind would blow through our entire booth and the dust would cover every nice thing we had. We would sell nothing all day, but that was business. I loved what we did, and I was always told if you love what you do, you will never labor painfully a day in your life.

It was in the fall of 1995 when I looked at those two babies growing up, taking steps, and starting to say words that I realized what I loved most was my time with them. At the time I didn't have much quality time for my family. We were so busy making a living, there wasn't a whole lot of time to make a life.

That is exactly how I was raised, hard work day in and day out. I was doing exactly what I had learned to do. The only thing that scared me was the fact that when we got married we vowed we would keep God first, then our family, then our career. How did this get so turned around?

What was the purpose of all of this? I used to question God, "If you are so real … where are you right now?" My bills were piling up, and we were working as hard as we could. No matter how hard we worked, it seemed like everyone else got paid except for us. Was this just part of owning our own business? I was tired, and my kids were being shuffled from sitter, to Nana's house, to the salon, to the park, to the rodeo, to the car seat. It was an absolute dead run every day of every week.

That winter was the hardest we had ever had. I wish I had known about Jim Rohn back then, and his theory of the seasons. I did not realize that the hard work from the summer had to get me through the winter, or I might not have spent the money I spent that summer. It was only normal to think that if things were busy, business would be getting even better. The reality is everything goes in cycles. We had a bill drawer in a file cabinet at our store that was so full we could not even close it. Dave would write checks to pay bills and then I would fret about how much he spent. There was never enough to get by at the end of the month.

During this dark and dreary winter our sales were low in the store, but I knew that the holidays would bring us some good revenue in the store. The scary thing was that you have to have money to stock the store in order for people to be able to come in and shop. The shelves were looking a little bare and the floor was emptier than it had been in months. I was scared, more scared financially than I had ever been. I even called an 800 number to help with the collection agencies. Dave and I had counseling with our banker and even an attorney on re-organizing our debts. We could not work any more hours that were traded for dollars. We had maxed out our earning potential.

I was so full of fear, resentment and doubt. Most of my friends were still going to college trying to figure out what they wanted to be when they grew up, and here I was 24 years old with two babies and over $200,000 of debt. I was working five businesses, trying to do the right thing, and no matter what I did, I would come to a dead end or a detour. That night it was well after midnight when I woke up crying. It is always scarier at night when you have fear. I called my mother-in-law crying and said, "I am exhausted and I just don't know what to do. They are coming to repossess our car tomorrow." She assured me that everything always works out. She was probably right, but right then I didn't know what to do. Words of encouragement are nice. However, nobody ever knows your problems like you do.

Dave didn't seem to be as stressed out as I was. He was very quiet and. of course, I was never quiet. I was thinking out loud and voicing my feelings with every breath. He was not joining in with his two cents.

I prayed for strength in the middle of those sleepless nights. I prayed for direction in what I was supposed to do, prayed for time with my kids and a strong relationship with my husband. Dave and I were passing in the hallway and very seldom ever at home. I wanted our lives to be simple again, and I wanted to have enough money to pay my bills. I think I even bargained with God, saying something like, "If you will fix my problems, I will never mess up again, and I will be a good Christian." What a fool I was to think that God would need me to bargain with Him. Did I forget that He knew my life long before I was ever even born? Did I not realize that He had a plan for me and all I needed was faith? Of course, I had forgotten that. All I could think about was my problems. I had forgotten that I was His child and that He wanted me to have all He created for me. I was scared and looking for all the answers on my own, but I had not looked to Him for help until I realized my way was not working.

During deer season, Dave had taken a break from the shop to go to his tree stand and scope out a deer. He was dressed in camouflage and had even painted his face to be able to sneak up and find the trophy buck. While he was out hunting a man stopped by and asked for the owner. I thought he was a friend and called Dave to come back to town from his tree stand to meet the man, but he turned out to be a total stranger. He had on a rodeo jacket and it said "Professional Bull-rider" with a championship and a year embroidered on the back. How would I know he was a salesman in disguise? Little did I know this day would forever change our lives.

It didn't happen that day—it was just the beginning. Do you remember the day you met your spouse? Did you know that very day that your life would change? Do you remember the day you met someone who influenced your life? Did you know it that day? I didn't either. In fact, I tried to reject the very thing God had planned for me. I usually chewed salesmen up and spit them out one salesman at a time. We had no money, no time, and definitely no extra energy to put into anything else in this store.

As the man tried to sell Dave some solid oak antique reproduction furniture for about $300.00 a piece, Dave glared at me through the lattice partition between the salon and the gift store. Dave explained that we had no money to invest, but the salesman was just persistent enough to stay there until he got our attention. He had been rejected by a furniture store on Main Street, and he had promised that store owner he would not leave Russell until he found a store that would take his furniture line. He explained that we could be exclusive for his dining tables and chairs, dressers, curios and hutches. Nobody else would carry what we had, and he was so sure we could make money. He would even leave it on consignment. No risk! Just sell it and make the profit. Wow! His three pieces of furniture did look pretty good in those big empty spots of our retail floor.

It took me only twenty-four hours to sell all three pieces of furniture and make more in commissions from those three curved glass curio cabinets than I had made all week. I was excited! Dave had made a new friend, and this friend was helping us make some extra money. The man came back through town with a truckload this time, and we bought six pieces. We could even haul these to our craft shows and make a whole lot more from a piece of oak furniture than a $20.00 candle. Thank God we had some money coming in.

Be careful what you ask for, because you will get it. Be careful who you take advice from, and most of all, be careful who you follow. There are people who cross your path for a reason, and many times you miss out on the opportunity God is putting there for you. Don't let fear keep you from the blessings that could come your way because of your current situation. I would have missed my entire calling if I hadn't been married to Dave Pitcock who had an open mind and was not quite as judgmental as I am. I guess you could say I had status, even though I was the girl who was broke. Spending money I didn't have to buy things I didn't need to impress people I didn't like who truly didn't care anyway. If I knew how little people actually even thought about me, I would have been amazed. The truth was that I looked good on the outside. I had the busiest salon in town and a very successful dance school. I was well-dressed and drove an average mini-van, although I couldn't afford to put a muffler on it. I looked good, but I was paddling like a duck underneath the water. I was fortunate enough to have someone explain this to me, and it forever changed my life. Dave didn't care so much what other people thought; he was looking out for the good of our family. I was always worrying about what people would say or what they would think.

One day the friend that I thought was bringing us furniture dropped off a video advertising a business opportunity and told Dave to watch it. He could get rich! I quickly explained to Dave, "Those things never work!" I think I told him it was probably produced by the Amway Corporation, and he replied, "What's Amway?" I didn't want to explain to him that Amway was one of the largest, if not the largest network marketing company in the world. I had been involved not once, but twice, beginning when I was just 14 years old. It was a great company with great products. I just never made any money!

I laughed, and we never talked about that video again. The winter was long, but we survived it. The bills were still high, but we were working hard to dig out. We were strong in faith that we would find a way to pay all of our creditors. I didn't want anyone to know that we were struggling and failing financially. So I continued to work and stay positive about the future. We did more shows, entered in more furniture markets, started setting the furniture out on street corners in other towns with banners on Sundays, and even traveled a five-state area helping other stores do what we had done in ours. We believed in this product and we could sell enough of it to get ourselves out of debt. Many weeks we would pick up a load of furniture with money we didn't have to spare and go on faith that we could sell it all in two or three days to cover the cost. We were not afraid of hard work; we thrived on it if it was helping us get out of debt. You have never seen hard work until you load and unload a trailer full of oak furniture in the hot humid weather of Missouri, then dust it with lemon oil only to unload it in Kansas, and watch the wind blow an inch of dirt on it again before you could get it in your store. Our dreams were big, and we believed that we would be successful. Someday, some way, we will be able to afford a new home. Some day, some way, we will be able to get a little nicer vehicle. Someday, some way I will be able to buy my kids a little nicer pair of shoes. My dream was to buy new clothes and not have to go to a garage sale for their clothing. My dream was to put a new front screen door on the house. I wanted nice things, and I knew someday things would change.

In February of 1996 Dave drove to Kansas City to pick up another load of furniture. I stayed at the store to make some extra money that weekend and had the kids there with me. Chance was colicky, and bless his little heart, he cried the first four months of his life. Dave's brother Scott went to Kansas City with him, and I remember they called home joking that maybe they could make a full-time living playing black jack. I wanted to beat them both. "Are you at the casino?" I asked. "I'm here with two screaming kids, and you are joking and having fun?" I was always worried when he called with an idea. Dave was the risk-taker in our relationship, and I was always hoarding every dime I could spare to save up for the next dilemma we might have. My goal was just to keep the lights on and not have the hot water shut off at the salon.

Sometimes the life of a mom is not as easy as some people might think. Not only do you have your own responsibilities, but it almost seems like being grounded from the things you like to do for fun until you get those little ones raised. I loved being a mom, yet I would find myself resentful of the person who got to go to the grocery store and keep her groceries in the cart while mine were flying out both sides of the cart and my kids were pulling each other's hair. I used to dream of a hot meal or a shower in the morning that wasn't interrupted with my motherly duties. I was losing that feeling of being independent and a successful business woman and I was feeling more like an absolute failure in every area of my life. I couldn't sleep through the night. I couldn't keep up with the house, the laundry, the yard, the car, the kids, and I had no time to do what I liked to do. I guess you could say I was living one hundred percent for everyone else and I had no balance in my life at all. No wonder things were such a train wreck. I learned a lot of lessons during this time.

Lesson Learned:

> *"Balance in your life is more important than the balance in your checking account."*

BARB PITCOCK

4

The Decision That Changed Our Lives

IT WAS THE SPRING OF 1996 when my life, as I knew it, was about to change. I would often wonder, "Why is this happening to me?" At a time when it was hard to find enough change to buy formula for the babies, or change at the toll booth, let alone make the car or mortgage payment, my husband informed me that he had found a way for us to become rich! Little did Dave know I had no belief in the so-called "home-based" business industry.

Dave was so excited as he explained the concept I had heard so many times. I didn't have the heart to tell him I had previously worked about a dozen companies and this was not a "new" idea. There are hundreds of companies out there and if you work once and build an organization of people that use the products, you get paid for the rest of your life with residual income that is money that comes in every month even if you stop working. This income is based on the products that are ordered through your network because you told someone about the product who in turn persuaded someone else, and this grows to create a consumer base for the company. Depending on the volume of products ordered, the commissions can be huge, and I had met millionaires who made their fortunes in this arena. There was no question that it is a brilliant concept. I just hadn't experienced the results that so many of them said you could experience.

My grandfather had been successful in several of these kinds of companies when I was growing up and even earned a free car. However that wasn't the case with the companies I had worked so hard for. I believed in it at one time; it was something I had tried since my sophomore year in high school. At this time in my life the faith I had that his little home-based business would be the answer to my prayers was slim to none. That week I had been on my knees praying that God would deliver us from debt. I prayed that I wouldn't have to leave our babies every day and go to a job that was paying me just enough to get by, and lately it wasn't even doing that. The answer I was looking for was not the answer I got, but today I can laugh about it.

I was furious to learn that Dave, the rodeo cowboy in blue jeans and boots who had a fear of people like most of us fear dying, was now the proud new distributor of a home-based business. He was very shy with an introverted type of personality. Dave would be the quiet guy that stood back and listened, not the first guy to initiate a conversation. And I had no idea where he had found the money, but it cost over one thousand dollars. He had purchased a "distributor" or sales kit and an additional $1000 in products, so he had spent $1,035.00 plus shipping and tax to get started—and in 1996 that was a tremendous amount of money. His friend had called weekly to see if we had watched the video he left with us and if we were ready to join the venture with him. Each week I assured Dave that there was no money in the checking account to join this venture with his friend. Obviously when Dave was in Kansas City he had found the money. I was thinking of all of the things I could do with that money, not knowing until later that he had borrowed a relative's credit card!

There was something about Dave that was different from many people. He had so much hope and he was full of enthusiasm about our future. I was quick to cut him right down to size and let him know that all those companies paint a pie-in-the sky picture to get you to join. He didn't let my negativity phase him as he smiled and put the video in our VCR, blaring loudly enough that I could hear it in the kitchen. As I did the dishes and wiped off the high chairs, I was letting him have it in my mind. Why would he spend the money and join something without me? I was stomping and fuming with anger and shock, since we had never had a fight in the few years we had been together. I bit my tongue until the end of the video as I watched this "infomercial king" persuade his viewers with a serious look and a phrase I had heard by so many giants in this industry. He said, "We'll see you on the beaches of the world …" and that's when I lost it! "We'll see you on the beaches of the world …," I mocked as I scrubbed the cheerios off of the tray and the ramen noodles out of the pan. "Wow! He sold you, didn't he?" I asked sarcastically.

It was a quiet night at the Pitcock house, but in the back of my mind the dreams I had years ago were stirring. What if this is it? What if this could work? I remember telling Dave I didn't care if he did it, but he was not to tell any of my friends, or clients from the salon, or dance moms from my dance school, or any of our relatives. I hoped it would work for his sake, but I wasn't going to get my friends involved in the next new thing smoking through town. It's too good to be true I thought, and I rolled over to try to get some sleep, with nagging thoughts of our drawer full of bills and the calls from creditors in the back of my mind. It was hard to sleep before with the anxiety of everything we had happening in our lives, but this new venture made it even harder.

The next night was the big meeting Dave had planned, and everyone was coming over! I was so concerned about helping him get his money back, I even called a few people, just because I felt sorry for him. I think my invitation went something like this, "You probably wouldn't be interested, but Dave joined this business for a thousand dollars. He is having a meeting tonight. Some big guy from Nebraska is coming if you want to stop by. If you're not interested, that is okay. I understand, but I thought I'd invite you over."

Possibly due to my great invitation, there was nobody there at 7:00, and at 7:15 we watched our friends drive by and stare at the empty driveway. I had invited my previous sponsor and his wife who drove by rejoicing that we were having a no-show. We had spent years together after he introduced me to a company one day as I was cutting his wife's hair. I could understand why they might not want to join another company. We had worked so hard together in the past as we struggled to achieve success, but were never successful enough to experience the fulfillment of our dreams and goals. It was tough to get your hopes up again and not to think about the past, but I thought they could at least come over and listen as I had done when they invited me to look at something.

The other young woman who was a "no-show" was my other colleague in that same business and was one of my best friends. She was circling our block to see if anyone had come, and suddenly came down the alley just as I was leaving to pick up the kids from the babysitter I really couldn't afford. I thought she was going to run over me when she failed to turn her headlights on until she was right upon my vehicle. I was so humiliated. I knew it would be this way for Dave when he joined the business and was rejected by people who didn't come to our meetings or made fun of our home-based business. I could not believe this was happening.

At the last minute I invited the nail technician from the salon to our meeting, hoping she would stay for the meeting. Dave called his mom to ask her to come, just to ease the embarrassment of having someone who was actually successful drive five hours to our home prepared to show the plan to the forty-plus people we had invited. Dave's mother joined us in his new venture, but Chris, my nail technician, didn't say much as she dropped off the salon towels and left quickly. I felt sorry for Dave, but part of me was doing the "I told you so" dance as we folded up the forty chairs and put away the drinks, cookies, and all the fine dishes I had put out to entertain. I knew better when I set it up, but with all of Dave's optimism, I wanted my home to look nice for our guests.

That evening we had the most important conversation of our career. When the big guy showed up to present this meeting, I thought at first that he was one of Dave's friends. There was not a "Slick-Willie" in a suit and tie look for this guru. The guy who came to present the business opportunity to us arrived in blue jeans, tube socks and a western shirt. I mention the tube socks because he took his manure-covered western boots off at the door. He had made a fortune in the industry in a prior venture. I felt comfortable with him, and there was an aura about him that convinced me he was real. I didn't feel the need to have him prove how much money he made. He was confident in the business he was involved in and eager to help us to get started making money. He turned the chair around and straddled it, sitting just a few feet from Dave and me and said, "Don't worry about tonight. You guys are just getting started." He asked us when the best time would be for him to come back. He mentioned that he had brought a case of promotional videos that explain how the business works to make you successful and gives information about the company we joined. He gave them to us to give away to our friends to help us launch our business. It was a good thing, because I couldn't imagine buying videos. After all, we had just spent more money to get involved than we had in all of our accounts combined.

This man made an investment in us that night. He may have had no idea it would pay dividends like it did, but surely his confidence in us was more than we had in ourselves. He started us in a way that we had no choice. Failure was not an option. We had to make this work. He made a commitment to come the following Tuesday back to our living room at the same time and said, "Get these videos in the hands of everyone you know. Some of your friends will have an interest. Sign them up and put them on your top level. The first ones involved could end up with million dollar spots because of the way the sales commissions are structured and you need to let them know that. Let them bring their friends, and we will help them get their money back, too. I'll see you next Tuesday!" He handed me an audio cassette, and told me to listen to it before I invited anyone else.

I didn't want to tell him my pre-conceived notions about audio tapes for motivational training. I had been in another company back in 1988 and had more audio cassettes than the entire music section at Walmart could house. I had listened to so many tapes to learn and implement the principles they claimed would lead to success, but for some reason this had never worked well for me. I couldn't imagine plugging in another tape. My previous failures were sending me signals saying "don't go there again." I resisted the negative thoughts in my subconscious mind, but this small voice in my head was saying "Barb, you spent money you didn't have. You invited every friend you had in the 80s and "sponsored" them to join a business to buy and sell products, and they didn't have any success. In fact, neither did you! You are a fool if you do this again! You don't have any time, you don't have any money, and if you go this route, you won't have any friends left either!"

It was hard to be positive, but I was drawn to this business in some way. What if this one would work? The previous businesses were never a scam. They were always good companies. I think it just wasn't the right timing. All of the elements weren't in place. Either everyone had already heard about them and there were too many people involved, or they weren't well-structured.

I had never seen Dave this excited about anything. Not only did I feel unsure of myself, but the guy was driving back all the way from Nebraska again next Tuesday. I was nervous and uncertain. I had a lot of responsibilities, including two babies, and listening to tapes was just one more thing I would have to fit in. He left a book called *The Magic of Thinking Big*. I didn't know how to break the news to the gentleman that busy moms don't have time to sit around reading a book all day. I had never been a reader and I wasn't about to start now. He suggested reading just the first chapter. Dave read it immediately, and I was resentful that he was sitting around reading. After all, I hadn't sat down all week. If I was a bit negative in my own way, it didn't stop Dave from doing everything he was taught by those who had introduced him to the business. He was "by the book" on everything they told him to do. He even started talking about dreams and goals and putting them up on our refrigerator. "Oh, no!" I said, "We are not pasting our dreams all over. My family will bust a gut laughing when they come over and think we are crazy. We are about to lose our cars, and you want to put a picture of a new truck on the fridge?" He didn't really care about my family and their opinions. He was focused on this business and he was on a mission.

Dave put the tapes in his truck and tried to preach to me each day, but I, being the network marketing expert from the past, didn't think I could be taught anything else. He for sure wasn't going to teach me anything. I had been involved in Amway, Avon, House of Lloyd, Mary Kay, Arbonne, Equinox, Christmas Around the World, and too many others to mention. My grandmother was a distributor for Fuller Brush and my grandfather actually earned a free car with Nanci Weight Loss System. I just couldn't bear the thought of another network marketing experience. I worked hard at most of the companies I had joined. I might have worked harder for the last few, but I didn't have the support from my sponsor.

One person came into the salon and signed me up for a $50.00 marketing kit, but I never heard much from her again. Many times distributors like her make the mistake of thinking that it's all about how many marketing kits they sell. But they also make commissions on that person's sale of products, creating a chain of sales commissions. The distributor should act as a sponsor by supporting the people who buy the kits and teaching them how to be good salespersons. If people only sell or buy the marketing kits and do little else, they become just another statistic of the many who join a network marketing company and end up making no money. I definitely did not want to be another one of those statistics.

My mother had two brothers who were always calling her about the next venture they found, and I was sure not going to be the person in our family that everyone laughed at and questioned about joining another business. All of these companies were good companies, and they all had great products, but in my mind the object was to become financially free. Financial freedom was my dream. I prayed for relief from the stress and our debt, but I wanted to send God a small note that said, "Wrong answer!" when this answer came. Little did I know this business could forever change our lives!

Five days later when I finally listened to the tape the man had put in my hands, I wished I had listened to it earlier. On it was a story that made inviting my friends very natural and actually kind of fun. I will never forget hearing this story. It made so much sense.

It went something like this: "Imagine waking up and there is a money tree in your back yard. This tree is covered in money, and there is plenty for you and all of your friends; but for the first day you can only invite four people to share in your fortune. As you pick off the money, it will replenish itself. Then those first four people can also invite some friends, but you have to keep it limited to those you care about the most. If you were standing in your nightgown getting your first cup of coffee in the morning when you noticed this tree, how would you react? Would you call your friends and say, 'I don't know if you would be interested? You don't have to come over, but there is money falling off the tree in my back yard. I can only tell four people. So I called you first, but don't feel bad if you aren't interested.'? Heck no, you wouldn't talk like that. You might say something more like this: "You are going to faint when you see what I just found. This is amazing! Get over here right now! What, you are busy? Stop what you are doing. It is going to blow your mind!"

What a difference when you believe and know that what you are offering is so good and that you will have a positive impact on the friend you are calling! The thing I was missing was belief. I didn't want my friends to get hurt. I didn't want to be embarrassed that I got them into something negative. I didn't want them to feel like they were being "got," and I didn't want to be getting them… I just wanted to make some money, and I needed some people to get involved. I psyched myself out prior to calling a friend in another town and I used the money tree story to get my enthusiasm up. My results changed immediately. It doesn't matter what you are selling or what you are trying to persuade someone to buy into. You must first believe that it is the best thing that could have ever happened to you in your lifetime. Not only do you have to have that kind of belief, you need to know what to say and to not say too much. I was the type of person that could go on for an hour without taking a breath. Dave was convinced the person on the other end of the phone had probably laid the phone down on their sofa and was dusting their entire house while I was getting winded from enthusiasm on my end of the phone. I said too much and I cured their curiosity. There was obviously no reason for them to come and sit through a meeting. I had told them all about it.

If you are in sales or marketing, you must find a mentor you can learn from. My mentor taught me a lot about invitations. You need to peak their curiosity, but don't cure it. You have to leave them hungry for information if you want them to come see what you have to offer. When you think about it, people tend to put up resistance and be defensive when you invite them to look at a venture for the first time. Most people are busy, financially strapped, have been in at least one home-based business before, and are skeptical. I was all of these, and yet I ended up a new distributor. How did that happen? If you were to ask most people who are new distributors, they weren't necessarily standing around with their hand in the air saying pick me, invite me to join you in your business. Most people are skeptical and are either too busy or they don't have the time and interest to put into one more thing. Many people do not have the money to get started in a business, and those who do aren't always willing to risk it. The ticket to getting someone to look at what you are doing is to tell them a story and for you to believe in it.

Think about this for a minute. I say to you, "I want you to come and look at a business." What did you feel?

Now think about this statement. "I have to tell you what happened. You are probably going to think I am crazy!"

Or say, "You won't believe what we did this week."

If someone offers to share with you a story or a joke, you draw near to them, eager to hear. However, if someone tries to sell you on something, your human instinct is to debate and find reasons not to do it.

You have to be careful not to get too excited and share all of the details. Less is more for your invitation. Just invite them and get a commitment. After you have an appointment, get off of the phone. Peak their curiosity, but don't cure it! You have to leave them hungry for information if you want them to come see what you have to offer. Once I learned this lesson my business forever changed. The forty-two people no-show meeting could have been the end of our story in that company, but instead it was the night that turned our business around. The tape I listened to was worth its weight in gold. I had found a mentor that I couldn't get enough of and I wanted every tape this lady had ever made. Dave, on the other hand, was listening to a two-tape set teaching him how to get our business started quickly. Some of us relate to stories, and others relate to philosophies. It takes discipline to listen and learn, but it sure does make a difference in your relationships, your income, and your happiness if you can find someone who inspires you to be excited about your life and have hope in your future.

A mentor is vital for your success in anything you do. This person should be someone you look up to who has had the success you desire and has achieved the results you want to achieve. Think of this person as your trainer or coach, and make sure you are learning from someone who has actually done the job you are pursuing.

I encourage people to find a mentor that they can relate to and to soak up all of their knowledge like a sponge. The tapes that Dave listened to shared some startling information he couldn't wait to tell me about. *Five years from now you will be the average of your five closest friends.* If we were to become the average of our five closest friends, it was obvious to us that we needed to find some new friends! That was hard, because I liked my friends. I looked at their income levels, their relationships, and their futures, and it was hard for me to swallow that this would be us unless we changed. I definitely wanted to go down a different road from where they were headed. I didn't have any other friends. Who would we do things with? A lot of changes were happening in our lives, and I prayed that it would be for the good.

5

Define Your Dreams

THE FIRST MONTH DAVE AND I WERE IN THE HOME-BASED BUSINESS that was his idea, I had a lot of growing to do. I had listened to some training tapes, but what truly got us both plugged into the system that turned our finances around happened during a road trip to deliver Dave's wholesale solid oak furniture to out-of-state stores.

No matter what you choose for a career, you need some training to get yourself on the road to success. The best training is usually not found in school but from your hands-on experiences and the lessons you learn from a mentor who is teaching you as you grow.

When we drove to South Dakota and Iowa together delivering furniture, we had the two babies in car seats that made it rough to listen to the information on training tapes, but somehow we managed to have quite a paradigm shift. The tapes were an eight-step series that took us from defining our dream to teaching others to duplicate this in our organization. This was not a new theory. It was the very training I listened to in 1988 and 1989 as I graduated from high school and tried to pursue a network-marketing career to help me afford my college education. It was hard to absorb this information and not have that syndrome of "here we go again," but this time I was ready for the information. This time I had a burning desire and a need for the finances I dreamed of achieving. There is nothing wrong with failing in business, because you learn so much with every failure. I felt like I was ahead of the curve as we listened to the training tapes, if only I could believe that it was going to work. Together Dave and I went through the steps and we followed their system.

The first step was pretty simple for me. It was to define your dream and get a burning desire for its achievement. I always warned Dave, "Don't fall in love with a dreamer." From the first night we met, and during the road trip we took to Kansas City and Missouri, I would take him off the beaten path to some gated community to see my dream homes. I am surprised he didn't get scared and run, thinking he could never afford something of that caliber. Not Dave. He was determined, and this was the vehicle he believed would help him get all of his dreams. At that time his dream was to rodeo full-time. He wanted to ride in the PRCA World Finals Rodeo. He drew out the arena, he visualized the Las Vegas event as if it was real, and he even imagined them calling his name. I believed he could do it, but I was scared to risk it. I didn't know how to tell him I loved him unconditionally, but it killed me to see him make a living on the back of a bull that wanted to kill him! I didn't want to steal his dream. I encouraged him by saying, "As soon as we make $10,000 a month you are free to quit working and hit the road!" He agreed.

It was hard for me to define a dream and not feel like a fool, because all that I could think about was my current situation. I was scared to get my hopes up, because what if it didn't work? The guy Dave was listening to had made millions of dollars, and he kept talking about our thoughts and how powerful they are. I was listening to tapes that I thought were so corny and I was feeling better than I had ever felt. As I was writing down my goals, the man on the tape mentioned some statistics that stuck with me every day. Ninety-nine percent of our thoughts are from the past, and only one percent of the thousands of thoughts in our mind each day are actually about the future. No wonder it is hard to dream. All that our minds can think about is what happened last time, or what came in the mail at noon, or what current financial or personal challenges you are facing. People don't realize that these situations are only temporary and there is always a rainbow after every storm. It's how we deal with these challenges and the thoughts that consume our mind that determine if we become successful or continue to struggle. The fears in our mind are often based on events that have happened in our past lives and truly have nothing to do with the present.

I set a goal to pay for day care and to be able to fix our front door. I dreamed of getting a new shower curtain ensemble and bathroom set and a fence that wasn't falling down. Yes, we made a lot of money at the salon and dance school, and Dave's furniture business could turn thirty or forty thousand dollars a month in inventory. But although we were moving a lot of income while being self-employed, there was never any left for ourselves. We were never home before dark, and we dropped the kids off each morning at day care before the sun came up. More of our income was going towards day care than there was for me to spend on necessities or things I wanted.

I was becoming more and more enthusiastic each day as I listened to those training tapes. The amazing thing was that we were paying $35.00 a month for two audio cassettes and I could hardly afford gas for my car. I had no idea how valuable those tapes were at the time. It was one more thing for me to be hung up about. I just tried not to think about the money we were spending and to believe that this would work. Every month we had to purchase a minimum of $100.00 in products that were for our own personal consumption and for any customers that ordered under our number. In addition to that, our overhead included the monthly training audios. I now think of the knowledge gained from this as getting a master's degree in network marketing. Many people go to school to get an education and never make the incomes that people are able to earn in the home-based business industry. Now that I know the value of the training, $35.00 is a low price to pay to be trained by experts in the field, but at the time, $35.00 was a bunch of money to me!

I would close my mind and do the exercises about my dreams and goals. For a minute I could almost imagine it so vividly that I forgot about the things that caused me worry. If money was no object, what would I do? What would you do? Just imagine someone telling you that you could make $30,000 a month and that you could meet the people that were making that kind of money. I threatened to streak down our local Main Street screaming and knock the mailman over as he handed me the check when my income hit thirty thousand dollars a month. Those thoughts had me out of my mind with excitement about what I had to do to make it work.

Everyone is different, but this exercise of dreaming and visualizing is the only reason people succeed in anything they do. It is what keeps you engaged in the action steps long after the excitement of beginning the venture has passed. It is the only reason I didn't pack up our box and get a refund the first night when nobody showed up at our meeting. I believe it is what makes or breaks people getting involved in their own business, because they are their own boss and they have to know what drives them to reach for their success. It is not like going to work and punching a clock. When you are your own boss you have to be driven by something that stirs you.

I started with some realistic short-term goals. I could not imagine what it would be like when we hit our first goal in the business and could take care of some of those old bills in the drawer. Or better yet, I imagined what it would be like to pay cash for groceries instead of using a check I hoped would not hit the bank until after the weekend.

When we set up our hand-made furniture and crafts in parks on the weekends, it wasn't easy. It was normally dark in the park and we had two babies with us. We always tried to beat the competition with our displays in order to attract the craft show attendees to our booth to sell our holiday décor or wooden benches. I still cannot believe how hard we worked, and especially on those days that we set up with a poor crowd showing or had no customers at all. Other weekends we would set up and sell out before noon. It's just business when you look at the traditional entrepreneur starting something with a goal to make some money. Most new businesses don't focus much on immediate results. People expect to spend money up front to make money in any business they start. The average business owner doesn't make a profit until he's spent five years of hard work building up his business. I was used to working hard in a traditional business. I had learned to spend money and sacrifice time and money in order to build something profitable. Why would I expect a home-based business to be any different?

This is what I found when looking at the average small, home-based business start-up cost and comparing it to others:

Start-up cost of Dave's woodworking business:

$5,000 in power tools and wood to start

$500 in advertising to get some customers

$1,000 a month in entry fees to set up for retail shows—no guarantees

Start-up cost of my salon in 1991:

$3,500 for the 175 sq. foot trailer house

$4,000 in training

$5,000 in inventory

18 months of eight-hour days at school

Some days I would make no money. Other days I would work ten hours and make $300 but I had to figure in overhead, day care, insurance, and time, which left me with about 30% of the actual earned dollar.

Start-up costs of a coffee bar Dave and I opened in 1995:

$3,500 for machine

$3,000 for tables and chairs

$350 for the neon sign (almost as much as a home-based business)

$1,500 in inventory and promotion

At the coffee bar in our little town some days were good. Others were slow. Add up the amount of $4.00 coffees you have to sell, less your expenses, to recoup your ten thousand dollar investment. Then try to hire an employee and afford to stay open. We put the coffee bar right in the middle of the building that housed the salon, the furniture, the craft store consignments, and Dave's wood-working shop was about fifty feet away in the back room of this old building. You could get your hair done, listen to the saws, smell the furniture stripper, and get a latte all while your perm was processing! What a delightful experience! Looking back now, it was called survival, and I have no idea how we survived. We had small businesses, and we started on our own without a lot of collateral.

I have talked to people who went to school and graduated owing $40,000 to $140,000 in student loans. One chiropractor that I talked to owed over $100,000 in student loans and borrowed that much again to open his practice, only to try and build up a base of clients and patients. No matter what your situation is, any business you open takes an investment of your time and your money. In most businesses you still have a job where you have to show up. Think about the time some of the top paying jobs require. Can you imagine being a doctor on call, or an attorney working on long cases that last for weeks on end? It's one thing to be in business for yourself and to be successful. It's another thing to leverage your time and your money to the point that you are truly free. I was learning the difference in what success meant to me. To each person success may mean a totally different thing. I learned to define success and pin point what it was that would make me tick.

Dave and I were totally different, but we both had the vehicle that would help us to reach our destination. Anything you do takes time and money. Most people do not have a lot of extra time or any money to spare. Where else can you start a business for less than a thousand dollars or even a thousand dollar investment and make your money back in the first month or two? What if it took a year? I never realized how fortunate I was to have an opportunity in my hands that allowed that. I was taught hard work was the only way, and I was not afraid of working harder. I had to learn to work smarter, instead of working harder. Leveraging your time was something I had always heard, and I was about to understand exactly what that meant.

The next Tuesday night came quickly and we had shown the video to several people. Some people thought we were crazy for joining something like that. I didn't get a lot of support from family. In fact, they laughed. My mom couldn't believe I had spent that kind of money and couldn't even pay my bills. I was nice and just kept her informed, even though I wanted to tell them that if they would support me, I wouldn't have to worry about money. My previous sponsor in another business was open to the idea after I approached him three times in one week, and did not give up until he agreed to at least watch the video. He said he would come to the meeting but wouldn't promise me anything. I was so enthusiastic and I told the story like I was taught—in a way that he couldn't resist. "Jeff, I know you think I'm crazy. We've done this before, but I gotta tell you what happened. Dave went to a meeting and joined the business without me, and I was so skeptical. We have no time, no money, and quite honestly, I have nobody else to call and approach. This is so different than anything I've ever seen. We have support that is unbelievable and training from people who are actually making twenty and thirty thousand dollars a month. You have to see this. I think we are going to get rich!"

The upline is the group of people who are directly above you in the business structure. These people are the people who benefit from your success and everything you are building. Therefore they should help you in any way and should support you in your business building activities. It's not always that way, and in a lot of companies I didn't have that kind of support. Knowing what I know now, I realize how important it is to have support from the people in your upline. It was so exciting to see that kind of support and training from those who were actually successful.

This company was so different from the others because there was no inventory, no door-to-door sales, no paperwork, and the most exciting thing to me was that the pay plan was structured different from anything I had ever seen. In most companies everyone you sponsor goes directly under you, and basically if you never sponsor anyone you never make any money, but if you sponsor a lot of people it all benefits you. In this plan, it was such a revolutionary concept, because your first four people went directly under you, but after that everyone else "spilled" to fill in under your first four friends. Therefore, those first four would benefit from everything you ever did. It was so exciting when I thought "Even my lazy relatives could succeed in this! It's a no brainer!" The other thing was that all you had to do to qualify for all the main bonuses, was to sponsor four people, and that was something that almost everyone could do. It was unlike most companies where you have to be continually finding people to enroll or you don't get paid.

I called my best friend and told her the same thing. "Tina, I know you must think I'm crazy after all we've been through, but we fell into something that has me so excited. I can't even sleep at night. Tina, all the things we dreamed about can happen with this plan. It has solved all of the headaches in network marketing! You owe it to yourself to at least look at it. If you have no interest, that is 100% okay, but it doesn't cost anything to look!"

I was optimistic this time, and I had confidence that people would show up at our meeting. We had a lot of seeds planted with potential people and had received some commitments. We hadn't used the whole case of videos, but we were definitely getting them out the door. We were showing everybody what we were doing. No profit is made on the selling aids, but purchasing them was an important investment to make to get our business off the ground. We mailed some to Nebraska and Kansas City. We called people from high school and some from college. We made a three to four-page list of people, and we added new names to the list daily. Dave would bring his tablet to bed with us, and every night we would brainstorm who we could call the next day.

That day Chris, the girl at the salon, gave Dave her credit card to join. She was the first person we recruited, and his mother faxed her application in the same week. I couldn't believe it. It was working for him and people were getting excited. Dave never said a whole lot, but when people saw him this excited about something they definitely gave him their attention. Some laughed, some flat-out said they weren't interested, and others had questions we couldn't answer. We told everyone to come to the meeting at our house. That Tuesday came and once again, nobody came to our house. I was amazed! What were we doing wrong? I was so upset. My roller coaster had been so high and now I felt like I was coming to a halt where they undo your harness and ask you, "How did you like the ride?" I was scared that nobody else would join, but that was not an option. Dave and I already knew exactly what we were going to do with the money. This had to work!

We went to the table and sat down with our list of dreams. Why were we doing this business? If we hadn't done this step, I think we would have quit. You have to know why you are waking up and going to work every single day of your life. You must define the very burning desire that will make you jump out of bed in the morning and keep you lying awake dreaming at night. What is it?

List on paper fifty things you would love to do in the next five to ten years.

Of these fifty dreams, which five are the most important to you?

6

Don't Let Anyone Steal Your Dreams

IT'S NOT ALWAYS EASY TO KEEP YOUR VISION when things are not positive in your current situation. One of the hardest things I had to learn was how to stay focused on my dreams and not let the distractions, the setbacks, or the disappointments stop me from pursuing my mission. I will never forget my little brother, who was in his early teens, came over to the house that first week, where he saw the photos of the new cars and homes on my refrigerator. I had tried to convince my family to get involved and most of them thought I was totally nuts. It was that month that our car got towed away by the repo company. The first thing out of his mouth that day was, "I thought your millionaire friend was gonna pay your car off for you? What happened to that deal?" I wanted to slap him, but I didn't. I loved him. He was my little brother. How could he be so mean? He couldn't have intentionally stuck a knife in my heart and hurt my feelings like that on purpose, could he? He must have heard some of the adults at my mom's house talking. After all, he was just thirteen years old. He didn't have any reason to be worrying about me getting my car paid off. I don't think he realized how passionate I was about this business and the desire I had to make it work.

Nobody knew that I was having sleepless nights of stress and worry over the hole we had dug for ourselves while starting those five businesses. I'm sure my family didn't realize that I sat up at night balancing my check book and crying as I looked in on those little babies and wondered if there was any chance that Dave and I could achieve our dreams and get out of our current situation. Nobody knows what you are going through. They just see things as they are on the out-side. We looked good on the outside! We had a good business. Never mind that we were there from sun up until sun down. We had good dependable vehicles to get us down the road hauling all of our home-made goods to the next show. We lived in a decent house and it was clean and neat. However, it was not our house. We had a rent-to-own agreement. Sometimes things are not as they seem. Successful peo-ple, who are busy with their careers, aren't always happy. If you think of a successful person that you know, compare them to this situation and think to yourself: Do they have debt? Do they work long hours? Do they have children? Do they have time to spend with them? Do they get to do what they want when they want, or does their business own them? We were successful, but we were on the road to nowhere working long hours without time to spend with our children or each other. The bank got its money, most of the time, and everyone else got paid, but that is not success.

Our neighbor lady was always home sitting on her front porch rocking her little ones in the swing when I would come home. In the morning she would be picking fresh flowers out of her perfect garden in her front yard. As I drove off to work, I would notice our front screen door swinging in the wind or a diaper blowing across the yard because some dog had dumped over our trash. I always compared myself to our other neighbors. I would compare my yard, my fence, my car, and how I kept up with things. What I didn't compare was my ability to survive and do whatever it took to never say "settle for mediocrity." I had big dreams, and I was sick and tired of being sick and tired. I was tired of watching the neighbors play in their yards as I worked an 80-hour week and then packed up to leave for a show on the weekend. I would dream of the day I could buy a new stroller or some brand new shoes for our kids, instead of being the first one at the garage sale in the nice area of town on Saturday mornings. Why not me? It was at that point that I got good and mad. My little broth-er had no idea what he did for me that day when he laughed at me and mentioned the car being repossessed.

I plugged in a tape and listened to it that day. It was titled, "Don't Let Anyone Steal Your Dreams." Our mentor in the business was from Chicago, Illinois. He drove a Rolls Royce and had a Lear jet that he had on standby when the car wouldn't get him to his destination quickly enough. His girlfriend drove a two-seater Mercedes 500SL, and he was very vocal about those friends who made fun of him. In fact, on one tape he talked about driving by a friend's house who had told him he would never make it, saying to himself, "How's K-Mart?" as he passed through the town where he grew up. "Yea," I thought to myself, "That's how all of the people who are telling me I'm crazy are going to feel when I pull up in that new car and move to a nicer neighborhood! Yea, that will be me laughing all the way to the bank some day if I can just get someone to join me in this venture." I was running out of people to call, so I did what the training said and decided to take their advice even though my way seemed easier. Instead of inviting people to a meeting they didn't want to come to, I decided to get in the car and go to them. I couldn't do it without listening to the Money Tree Story, of course. That always got me pumped and ready—and not thinking about the fear of rejection.

I decided my first stop would be the lumber yard. Dave and I had an account at the lumber yard for our craft supplies we used each month. We could cut out one hundred fifty snowmen on Monday and sell them all by Friday, so we were good customers of theirs. This was a scary stop because the owner and his wife were very successful, unlike many of the people I had tried to talk into coming over to my house in an attempt to save them. I was going for broke, so this was definitely a couple on my "chicken" list. I know I was sweating even though it was late February and cold as ice outside. I walked into the store, asked a kid who was one of several in their big family for the store owner, and entered his office. The paneling was out-dated, and I still remember the lines in it thinking, "I wonder why they don't fix it up since they have a huge store out there."

His dad owned many businesses just a few miles from Russell. If this guy would get in, everybody would do it! I hardly took a breath. I just went into my spiel ... "I know you are going to think I am crazy, because I can hardly believe it myself. You know how hard we work. Dave and I don't have a lot of time or money to do anything extra on top of what we are doing, right? Well, Dave and I fell into something, and I think we are going to get rich! I've been in several companies before and swore I'd never join another one, but Dave got us involved, and we are already making money. This is the most amazing thing I've ever seen in my life. I only have a minute, but I wanted to give you and your wife a chance to get involved on our top level. You were one of the first ones I thought of." (That was true, but 46 people later I finally got the nerve to go there.) He didn't say a thing until I finished. Then he said, "My wife will kill me! We were in another deal, and we really got burned, but if you can convince her, I'm in!"

"Wow," I thought. "He wants to look at it, but his wife is going to shoot us down." What should I do? I went home, as fast as I could, and called Dave to let him know he had to get back to town. Bert, our sponsor was on his way from Missouri, and he was a fairly quiet guy, definitely not one who wanted to do the presenting, but Dave believed him. So why couldn't they go do the meeting together? I set it up for 7:30PM, and I told them how excited our prospect was for them to come.

This couple had just built a beautiful new home on the edge of town. At 7:30 Dave and Bert headed to the meeting. I was home with the babies praying that all would go well with the guys at the meeting, and she wouldn't skin them. How would they convince her? After all, we are talking about two bull-riders going to the home of two highly educated, successful people. She was finishing her degree in teaching, and he was the son of a multi-millionaire many times over. It was a long night, and as I waited, I worried. What was taking them so long? Three hours later I could hear the laughter in the driveway as that noisy furniture-hauling diesel Ford truck was turned off and the doors slammed. I couldn't believe it! These two cowboys walked in with not just one application, but five!

Dave and Bert had managed to sponsor the couple who got so excited after seeing the video that they immediately called four of their closest friends. Their four friends all gave their credit card and social security cards right over the phone. How did they do it? The only reason I urged Dave and Bert to go in my place was because I was scared of the wife. I thought I was a natural born salesperson who could talk to anyone, and here they came back with five applications after a one hour presentation and a couple hours of conversation! I almost had a heart attack! It was the last day of the month and the end of the month was when bonus checks were figured. There was no Internet and there were only so many phone lines available. We hooked up our fax machine and started faxing in applications! We were in the money now! I was excited.

Excitement and belief that the business would work had created more income in that one hour than I normally made in take-home pay in an entire week. The new couple had four people and I was just getting my third position filled with their application. How could we let them pass us up? We were on fire, and we were ready to get the next person. This was so much fun!

I had a lot of videos that I sent out, and if any of those people would be interested, that might be a possibility for our number four. It had been so much fun sponsoring the couple from our "chicken" list, I decided I would send one to my rich uncle. In fact, Dave and I decided we would just get in the car and go see him! We loaded up and drove three hours from home to Wichita, Kansas. My mom's brother was always successful and lived in a nice cul-de-sac. He made a fortune with his boss, who was a real-estate guru. We drove into his fancy, gated neighborhood with our two small babies and our video. He was very nice as he watched the video and talked about the problems he and my grandpa experienced with their weight-loss company. His wife was not excited that he was looking at another company. She mentioned their neighbors and friends who were so upset about the company they built because they thought the company had changed all the rules on them. I remained enthusiastic as I encouraged them to think about this and take a position in our downline so they could get in at a good spot. I was doing all I could to get them signed up. They showed some interest but did not join that night. My uncle was the authority our entire family looked up to. My mom, as a single mom raising five children, always consulted my uncle before she made any decisions. I just knew he was going to join! If he would join, Mom would follow before we knew what happened.

A few days went by and our group was starting to grow on its own. My days were busy before, but now I woke up to tapes, did my motherly duties, went to work for eight or ten hours, picked up the kids, took them to a new sitter or to Nana, and then we headed out to find someone to show this video to. It was tough to leave them every night, but Dave and I had made a commitment. Our commitment was that we would show this plan three to five times a week personally until we replaced our income. That month of February we ended with three personally sponsored recruits we call executives. The total in our group with our friend who sponsored four, and Dave's mom, who had sponsored two, grew those nine to a total of twelve, and we didn't even know all of them!

It was a long winter at the craft store and the haircuts always slowed down in January and February when it is cold in Kansas. Thank goodness we had a check coming soon so that we would be able to pay some of our bills. I was hoping it would come soon and praying it would clear the bank! With twelve people in our group, we were still working to get our fourth "personal" or recruit signed up.

Finally, my sponsor from the grand-daddy-of-them-all network marketing companies came over to the house with his wife. He and his wife had been friends of mine for several years prior to my moving to Wyoming with Dave. We had gone to function after function together. I could remember driving home with him from the Kansas University campus after doing cosmetic parties for all of the sorority girls on campus. He had taken me to see Zig Ziglar at Wichita, Kansas when I was just nineteen years old. I was excited that this couple was serious about it, and they committed to take our last position on our top level. We finally had our four! That month when we had sponsored a total of the maximum of four people with Chris, Cindy, Russ, and Jeff on our top level, the next three people we sponsored, "spilled" over to fill the spots of people under us. They happened to spill under the manicurist who hadn't done much in the business. Since she was single and very attractive she had a busy social life. Nightly she was being bombarded with negative people who were sucking the life out of her. She was scared to ask anyone else after the first person she sponsored who had joined from pure excitement at her manicure table. The woman just gave her the credit card and said "put me in." She managed a successful bar and restaurant in town. That night when the woman went home excited about her new venture, her husband demanded that she get out. He said these kinds of things do not work. Chris took that seriously and was scared to ask anyone else. The great thing was that it didn't matter. We had people spilling into her group, and as my friend, I could assure her there was no way to lose. She was going to start earning commissions as people ordered the products.

The company we were involved in had a limited top level. There are a lot of great companies out there, and every compensation plan varies. In most companies if you never sponsor anyone, you never have the ability to earn a bonus check. The way this one worked was very intriguing. It was a 4 x 7 Matrix, which didn't mean much to me, except I understood that everyone you sponsored after the first four would "spill" into your group under the ones that joined before them. This group of people would form an organization called your "downline." Some people might end up with a downline that was growing from the "spillover" even if they only bought and sold products for themselves but never sponsored anyone. At first that's what got me excited. I thought we would just get in, sit and let our upline spill us full. Once I realized our sponsor joined the same night Dave did, I got a little nervous about waiting for a spill. We didn't have time to wait. We needed to make some serious money, or we were going to have egg on our face in our home town because we had five businesses that were barely treading water.

We made a commitment to build our business no matter what. If people said no, we learned to say "next." It was not up to me to convince them. It was just up to me to find three or four people who had a vision. Some joined, some joined and quit, and others joined and did nothing. Everyone bought products, and that was good because the only way to make an income was from the movement of products.

Lesson Learned:

> *"Focus on new blood. The new blood is the*
> *lifeblood of your business."*

7

Don't Let What Others Think Keep You from Achieving Your Dreams

DAVE AND I GREW UP IN RUSSELL, KANSAS. Being from this small town made it tough not to think about other people and what they were saying about you. My favorite definition of status put me in denial that I ever had it, but I did, and I had a serious case of it.

Status:

Spending money you don't have on things you don't need to impress people you don't like who really don't care anyway.

It was mid-March and our business was really starting to build. I was so thankful that it was going to work. There are three days that stand out vividly in my mind from that first year. One was the day Dave joined and had a meeting that nobody attended. The second day I will never forget was the day that Uncle Frank called. Dave hollered at me to come to the phone. Uncle Frank had called and wanted to visit with me. This was amazing! He was actually calling me back! I remember sitting on a warm radiator in the hallway of our old Victorian home, juggling my kids as they crunched up Ritz crackers on our hunter green carpet. Brooklyn was on the floor, Chance was on my lap, and I held the phone under my chin as I rocked him back and forth, nursing him and trying to keep Brooklyn happy. Uncle Frank sounded very serious as he encouraged me to listen, "Barb, the company you are in is a scam, and the Securities Exchange Commission (SEC) is going to shut it down! You need to get out. Get out now, and try to get your money back. The guy you think is so great is an ex-con for credit card fraud, and he's been in prison! You must get out right away before anyone else gets involved." He was serious and had me scared to death. I felt sick. My stomach was rolling.

We had just gotten a notice that our first check for $899.00 would arrive any day now. According to customer service we had close to fifty-nine people in our group, and we had only sponsored seven. What should I do? I looked at Dave, and he was curious as to what could possibly be wrong. I told him the news, and he immediately called our sponsor and our upline from Nebraska. Before long we were on the phone with the company, and I asked for the top leader in our organization. Of course he was not available to talk. I thought my call was urgent enough I could get through, but evidently we had to be making the big bucks to get through to him. They put me on the phone with his assistant.

That day I learned a very valuable lesson that kept me from quitting for the second time. It seemed like every day I would go through this emotional roller coaster of I love it, I hate it, I love it, I hate it, I love it. I immediately had "word vomit" as I panicked on the phone and couldn't stop talking to the young assistant about everything I had heard about our mentor being an ex-con. His assistant tried to settle me down as he assured me it would all be okay. "It is true, but there is nothing to worry about! Your mentor made some poor decisions in his life and lost his freedom for a few years. It was then that he began reading personal development books and turned his life around."

The kid on the phone poured his heart out to me about the owners of the company and their integrity. The assistant told us his story of how our mentor and this company had changed his life. He explained that as an independent distributor our mentor had created millions of dollars. Prior to joining this company, the assistant was a waiter living in a run-down apartment. He persuaded me to have thick skin, and understand that all MLM opportunities go through scrutiny during different times in their careers. He said that our company was being scrutinized by the SEC, because people were making such tremendous incomes. He said that we basically had two choices. We could trust our mentor and continue to build our business by taking advice from someone making $150,000 a month, or we could listen to our friends who couldn't make that in a year. There was nothing he could do but assure us that he was still building his business, and he encouraged us to do the same. However, *The Wall Street Journal* had an article in it that month about our company and the investigations it was under. I could not believe this was happening.

I went to the backyard to let the kids play so I could have a break to ponder the things I had been told. I watched Brooklyn swinging on the swings as Chance tried to stand up and walk around the yellow plastic slide that wound up to her wooden loft of the swing-set. He was such a handful of energy. At six-months old he was finally starting to sleep a little and not cry so much from his colic. I loved playing with them in the backyard. They were so close in age, it was almost like having twins. I sat there on the edge of the swing praying that things would work out for us. Each day as I dropped them off at the sitter, it was getting harder and harder to leave them. Brooklyn was singing songs and saying full sentences while she ran around like a big girl, although just eighteen months earlier she was less than five pounds and all I could ever want. With Chance coming so quickly after her, I used to wonder how it could get any better than it was right now, and if I could ever be that happy with a second child being born. The minute Chance was born my life changed. The miracle of these two beautiful babies was so much to be thankful for. I had healthy children, a wonderful husband, and I dreamed of our future together raising our family. I reflected back to the days when life was so much slower as I sat at home in the rocking chair waiting for Dave to get home on Friday nights.

Now my life was a whirlwind of paying bills, doing housework, teaching dance classes, going to craft shows, working full days at my salon to give people haircuts and chemical treatments while running a coffee bar and consignment store, and returning to two babies who needed me at the end of the day. There wasn't much time left for Dave and me, and that was the part that I missed so much. Now that we were in this business, we were excited about something that could give us back our time. I wanted to cry, but I couldn't dare let my kids see me sad. I pushed them on the swings and sang the Barney song with Brooklyn as she giggled, "I love you. You love me. We're a happy family. With a great big hug and a kiss from me to you, won't you say you love me, too?" That crazy purple dinosaur had her convinced that he loved her, and it seemed like every mom in America was singing it along with their kids. Maybe Barney was in network marketing? I don't know, but whatever he did for a career couldn't be nearly as stressful as the rest of the world when he wrote those lyrics.

It made me laugh, and they made me smile. No matter what happened, I was one lucky momma.

I noticed the guy from the lumber yard was delivering some goods to the lady across the street with the beautiful yard I always admired. I could tell he was telling her about the new business venture we were in together, and that she should join us. I slid down the side of the house so I could listen to their conversation just in time to hear her inform him of the fact she watched the city put disconnect notices on our doors and the repo company take our cars away. Her husband worked for a very well-respected oil company, and he would never allow her to do something like that. She urged him to think about what he was doing. I watched him get in his delivery truck and drive off, and I started to cry. Why was this happening? Why me? Was I doing something wrong, or was it just part of the test to see if I really had what it takes to make it? I wasn't sure I could handle much more and I was worried about Dave. He had never done anything like this. In fact, he didn't even know what network marketing was until two months ago. He was getting a whole new education on the realities of the business, and this is exactly what made me so skeptical about it in the first place.

It was a little late to worry about getting our friends involved, now that fifty-plus people were coming to the local Elks Club that next week to meet the "Big Guy!" from Nebraska. I had my attorney coming, our car salesman was coming, and my salon radio ad salesman had joined just because Dave handed him an audio cassette. In fact, the ad salesman left the salon, drove five miles out of town, turned around in the median, and came running into the store saying, "I've waited all of my life for something like this to come along!" Dave made it look so easy and everyone he talked to had an interest. Why was I so emotional about the whole thing? The difference between Dave and me is that he had no doubts. Doubt never entered his mind. Therefore, he was like ignorance on fire, and it was working for him.

That night Dave went to do a meeting and he never missed a beat. He drove to do a meeting about two hours west, and I drove to Salina, Kansas, just one hour east. I took the two babies and my mother-in-law with me. We did our meeting in the basement of a Salina hospital because the room was free. The two people at the meeting were in, and nobody they invited showed up. I could relate to them and encouraged them it could go from zero to 59 in a month, but they had to show the plan, even if they went to the people themselves. They laughed at me as I told them about my month. They must have believed me because they set a meeting for me to come the next Tuesday, and I agreed. It was a long drive home, but a good one. This gave me an hour to listen to tapes and try to make some positive deposits after the negative day that I had just experienced. I listened to the same tape, and I heard a whole different story this time. I guess I needed it pretty badly. This was becoming my favorite title, "Don't let anyone steal your dreams!"

I waited at home for Dave to see how his meeting went. He mentioned that some people had questions about the scrutiny, but there were about fifteen people at his meeting, and all of them were fired up about the future they had ahead of them. This roller-coaster ride was working its way back to the top. I felt pretty good that night as we laid there talking until the early morning hours. I couldn't sleep. Dave couldn't sleep, so we just got up!

8

Action Cures Fear

SPRING WAS COMING, and the sun was beginning to shine a little bit in between the cold and windy days. We still had days of sleet and snow, but they melted faster now. It was nice to be able to go outside for awhile and occasionally get the kids to day care without having to warm up the diesel truck for an hour before we left.

Bob Dole was coming to town and planned to announce his candidacy for presidency of the United States. He was a native of Russell, Kansas and his niece was a good friend of mine who also owned a salon in town. With Bob Dole's approval we printed up shirts, pins, caps and anything else we could put his name on to attract the people into our gift store. We were so excited that he agreed and he even helped us get the presidential seal on our shirts. Dave was headed to a big screen-printing company and had three or four ideas of what we would put on the shirt. I thought it needed to be a gold presidential seal that looked like a medallion and most of the others thought that a red, white, and blue design would be fine.

I happened to be visiting with my dance school assistant. She had taught for me the last two weeks of my pregnancy with Chance. She was a friend from elementary school I used to slumber party with, and her parents were good friends of Dave's family. We exchanged our ideas about the campaign, and she informed us that her sister had just married a guy from back east who was good at printing T-shirts. Immediately, I thought to myself, this is going to be a huge idea. We should just keep the business local instead of driving thirty minutes away to Hays, Kansas. We decided to get the ball rolling on some shirts.

Within a couple of weeks we had over 2,000 shirts. We put some money down and agreed to pay the remainder as soon as we sold them. The big day was coming soon and we would head to Topeka for Dole's announcement there. Nobody else would think of this! We were so excited about the campaign! Helping us elect a local president would make Russell boom again. We were on the corner of Russell Main Street, the Metropolis. Russell had a population of 3,500 at that time. One of my craft consigners made Bob Dole dolls and some home-made jewelry. We put out red, white, and blue banners and did all we could to get people in the door. We even hired a local woman to help tend to all of the customers coming in. She was a marketing genius. She would sell the souvenirs, rearrange the store and sometimes even decorate the outside of the store. Maybe it was the book we were reading, *The Magic of Thinking Big.* I had no idea how everything was turning around, but it was.

We packed the truck and trailer to head for Topeka, Kansas and the big Bob Dole announcement. Along with Dave and me were our moms, his brother and uncle, my four brothers and sisters, and of course, our two babies. We had newspaper route holsters for them to roll the shirts in and walk through the crowd saying "Get your T-shirt!"

It was the night before the announcement and security wouldn't let anyone near the building where the announcement was scheduled. We had to wait for the next morning to even get permission to enter the building. That morning we were there by 4:30AM People were lining up at the doors for the announcement at 8:00AM As the security guards came to set up, I assured them that we needed a good spot since we had conversations with Dole's office who gave their approval to sell the souvenirs. The guard could have easily told me "no," but somehow we ended up right at the entry way at the back of the coliseum.

It was a very fast crowd and they came in like a herd of cattle. My mom and mother-in-law, Cindy, were selling shirts; Brooklyn was on Traci's hip behind the tables, and Chance was fast asleep in his little rocker. In all of one hour, and we had sold most of our inventory. The only inventory we had left were T-shirts in small and children sizes and a few caps and buttons, but we were headed to Iowa the next morning. The total inventory remaining was about $3,000 in retail. That meant we had a cash bag full of money to take back to our supplier; we had sold $17,000 in merchandise in one hour! We counted the twenty dollar bills at a local hotel as we rejoiced in our success from Dole's announcement.

Our moms bundled up the babies and headed back to Russell as we hit the road to Iowa with Dave's brother Scott who worked for us at the shop, and his Uncle Art. Scott and Art were blown away by the sales, and we generously paid them for helping. We rented a van and drove all night to get to Des Moines. We found some Dole fans waiting, but the sales were nothing like it was in Kansas. We had ordered more shirts with the profit we made after paying the bills for the cost of the shirts sold in Kansas. This time we would make smart business decisions, spending none of our profit and re-investing it all in inventory. After we sold some merchandise we drove home to get ready for Dole's appearance in Russell, which was scheduled for the last day of March.

The month flew by. Because of spring break the salon busy with kids, and I spent any breaks I had on the phone making arrangements with the gift shops in towns where Bob Dole planned to appear next. I was amazing myself with my successful phone orders for Bob Dole items of several hundred dollars each day. I realized that we could greatly benefit from this opportunity. I even encouraged Dave and Scott to take the Bob Dole shirts to the Kansas City Market with the furniture Dave was taking there that week.

The Kansas City Gift Mart has a wholesale market for buyers from stores all over the nation and was held once a year. We decided that year to get a booth at market. It was a very expensive entry fee, but brought us business from store owners all over the Midwest who wanted to purchase items for the summer and fall. With the election coming soon I thought that wholesalers there would also want some shirts that could be sold along with the furniture Dave built. Dave and Scott had a blast selling both furniture and T-shirts and got many new accounts, including an entire chain of Hallmark stores.

We shipped off the inventory each week and paid our expenses as we went. Almost everyone was selling out the shirts quickly and re-ordering with rave reviews. Our integrity was most important, of course, and the customers all seemed happy until a woman from a Hallmark store called me from less than an hour away to ask me how the shirts were manufactured. After creating a store display she realized that the royal blue and gold presidential seals had turned to yellow and purple. It wasn't just the fading that concerned her, but that the pile all bled onto one another when placed in the sun of their front window display. I told her that I was very sorry, and advised her I would talk to Dave and get them replaced right away. This wholesale business to retailers was our livelihood, and we had to make them happy.

Dave did research on how the shirts were made and found out that they used was basically a process of heat application for the seals, which explained the poor quality of the T-shirts. Because the technology used on the first batch of shirts was like ironing on the decal, the decals were fading. The businesses selling these shirts as souvenirs wanted to make sure they had happy customers. Dave believed we must get a better quality. On our next order he made sure to order enough to replace the faulty T-shirts at our cost. He then found a screen-printer nearby who could guarantee the T-shirts, which seemed like the right thing to do in order to give our dealers a high quality shirt. The shirts would not be in for a week or two, and our local friend who had supplied the faulty shirts had taken a long vacation to the mountains. There wasn't time before our deadlines with our stores to try to find him to inform him of our plan.

In any business your integrity and the way you serve your customers is of utmost importance. Dave and I were committed to these customers and would do whatever we had to do to make them happy. Even if it meant we didn't make a profit from this first order, we knew they would see us at the next market. Dave was anxious to replace their shirts with good quality so they had them in time for the Dole campaign coming to their areas.

On a Wednesday afternoon in the salon, Dave's mom came to get the children. While she was there the sheriff walked in. At first I thought he wanted a haircut since I regularly cut his entire family's hair, but he had a paper in his hand. Since I was finishing with a client, I asked Dave to come out from the back room so he could sign the paper. I wondered what it could be about. I couldn't imagine who would be taking legal action against us. We were finally getting caught up with our finances. I was shocked to learn that the local T-shirt vendor was upset that we had taken our T-shirt orders to an out-of-town screen printer who offered better quality shirts. He claimed that our going out of town was a breach of a verbal contract and was filing a lawsuit for fifty-thousand dollars in damages. I could not believe it!

Rumors started to fly that we would soon lose our home because this vendor would take all we had. He had married into a family with a lot of wealth, and they had hired the most powerful attorney in town. This attorney was also Dave's mom's attorney, but we were too late to have him help us now. We were shocked! Fifty thousand dollars! This was a huge amount of money to us. We had already spent more than that within our first few months of working with him. How could he do this? I had tried to keep peace by not complaining that his equipment was "small-town" start-up equipment. We had asked him about the possibility of screen-printing after the first complaint, but he said the equipment was very expensive. Now there was nothing I could say or do, and Dave was furious about this action. I prayed that there was a solution to this allegation. I felt paralyzed with fear and shock that this was happening. I had never heard of someone taking a legal action like this. We didn't know what to do.

We found an attorney about thirty miles away who might be able to compete. The Dole announcement in Russell was just three days away. I couldn't even stand the thought of selling the T-shirts now. I wanted to burn them all and forget the whole mess! We were scared, and at the age of twenty-three and twenty-four, we had no idea what to do in a situation like this. It seemed as though success was coming quickly, but we were not strong enough to handle what it was dealing out as it came.

I was terrified to see an attorney, but we went. He wore a huge white cowboy hat and sat behind a big cherry desk. His office was filled with pictures and plaques of his many accomplishments, including running for a government office. He asked us all of the questions he needed answered and charged us a $2,400 down payment just to get started. We didn't have the money but we wrote the check out of fear and knew we would sell enough furniture and shirts in the next few days to pay for it. I remembered that we had a check coming from our new marketing business and that would help out with this unexpected expense.

I went to the Bob Dole candidacy announcement in Russell by myself while Dave worked the store. I sat at the table surrounded by T-shirts and keepsakes. I was not enthusiastic about it anymore, but I had to sell them in order to pay for their cost. I had to admit that the shirts from our new supplier were much more attractive, but the thought that I had upset my friend's family in our home town made me want to hide them all under the table. I couldn't handle anyone being mad about this. I wanted to fix it, and there was no way that I could. Obviously, I attracted just what I thought. Most of the people there weren't nearly as excited as I thought they would be, and I packed up my shirts one by one in brown boxes, hoping to never unpack this stuff at a booth again.

Just as I packed up my last box, Dave came running into our home town high school gym where I was at our booth. He was dancing like a crazy man. He had a large priority mail envelope in his hand, and inside of this envelope were a letter and a check. The letter congratulated us for sponsoring our first person to join, and the check was $899.00 for the month. We waited six weeks for the first checks to come and had built this on total faith. I couldn't believe it was real! We hugged and laughed as he gave me the check and said, "You can go put this in the bank!" The check had to be endorsed by Dave, because it read, "Payable to David Pitcock." Of course, my name was nowhere on it. It was his business, since I didn't want anything to do with it when he signed up!

I was throwing T-shirts in the truck as fast as I could and getting out of that school like we were having a fire drill. I went through the drive-through at the bank that had re-possessed our car, just to see if the check would deposit, and it did! Then I went around to the front door of the bank, parked my truck, and walked up to the teller to see what it would feel like to get that many hundred dollar bills from one check. As I was walking out of the bank with my envelope full of cash, I made a decision to go to the drive-through of the bank we had recently switched to. I felt the cash, and thanked God that it was real. Then I deposited it into the new account to cover our attorney's fees and quickly drove to the shop to celebrate with Dave.

We were excited one minute and scared to death the next. The attorney's fees were covered, but we knew this legal battle was going to be long and drawn out. The attorney fees were more than we could believe, but if we didn't have an attorney, we feared we might lose our home. We were renting our home with an option to purchase, and I worried about losing the equity we had in the purchase contract, and about being out on the street with my kids. What would happen if we lose the lawsuit? I was so scared. I would lie awake worrying about losing our business and wondered what the outcome would be. It is truly amazing what fear can do to your attitude about a business, and it is all reflected in your profit when you let that fear take over. I felt like I was paralyzed when I let fear take over my thoughts.

There were good things happening to us in many areas of our lives. We just had to find a way to conquer the battles in our minds. It was tough to go and do a meeting about financial freedom and health and wellness products when you didn't know much about nutrition other than the fact that a box of pills had just arrived. Our box was at the salon, and Dave was unpacking everything in our kit. We had been involved a little over three weeks and we were just receiving our starter pack with all of the products. There was a customer in the salon who asked Dave what was going on and he informed her of our new venture. She left excited like everyone he talked to and he put a video in her hand.

That night it was late when we got home, and we were just sitting down at the table when the doorbell rang. A farmer I was not familiar with stood in the doorway with his wife, who looked like the girl from the flower shop downtown. This was the customer Dave had approached earlier today with the video. They walked in with an application and check in hand. Dave asked the farmer, "So, what do you think?" The farmer replied, "I think if it takes a thousand dollars to teach my wife a financial lesson, I'll prove to her that these things don't work." He wrote out the check, shook Dave's hand and proceeded to the door. Dave assured them that if they would listen to the tapes, it would work. He handed them one of the sets that we had purchased so they wouldn't have to wait three weeks to receive their tapes. They left, and once again, Dave had sponsored another "personal."

We were now "Gold," which meant that we had sponsored eight people. Every time you hit a pin level, you changed a color. What a novel idea. This title was gold, yet in our eyes we were far from anything sparkling. We were in a storm of emotions and had no idea what to do. We went for a drive so the children would stop crying, and we could visit.

This was the first night we had been home together in many weeks. I noticed a card above Dave's visor in his truck. It was a business card with a bold black message on it. It read "Action Cures Fear." Dave encouraged me to stay faithful and that everything was going to work out. He was praying that he wouldn't just run over the T-shirt vendor in the street the next time he passed him, but he knew that there was no lawsuit or any obstacle that was bigger than us. He could tell me that all night long, but for some reason I could not stop worrying. I didn't want to lose my home or have any more failures in our home town. "We must take action every time we get scared, Barb. We can do this. We just need to keep showing this program," Dave said. I found it hard to find the energy every single night with all of our worry and the day-to-day grind.

I mentioned to Dave that I was getting burned out, and it wasn't coming in fast enough. It was then that he stopped the truck and said,

"Would you do it for $10,000 a month?" Yes, I would do it for ten thousand dollars a month, but I needed to see it first. From then on, there were no more excuses. We were on the road every night. I would cry and tell him how exhausted I was as we kissed good bye in the doorway, each of us heading to a new town to do a new meeting, going our separate ways every night of the week. Our kids stood at the doorway crying "Please don't leave!" and I would promise them that mommy was going to do a meeting so that I could take them to meet Mickey Mouse at Disneyland. We would walk out to our cars and high-five in the driveway. "I'll do it tonight for ten thousand dollars a month!" we would chant. Every night for ninety days straight that was our motto, and we believed it would soon happen for us like it had for the people in all of the success stories in the video we watched.

I do believe that if you take action it helps you overcome your fear. The longer we sat without doing anything, the worse the fear became. It is not easy to go and do the right things when you have adversities in your personal life. It is hard to be enthusiastic about anything when you have financial struggles and wonder how you are going to make it. You can't focus only on the current situation and expect to get a different result. You must stay motivated with the vision of what it is that you desire the most, as if you already have it.

Believe it—and you can achieve it. Doubt it—and go without it. This was the tagline on our T-shirts that we wore to the first meeting that came to our area. We lived by it, and we taught our friends and family in the business to believe it.

What are the action steps that you can take immediately to keep you from being stopped because of fear? List the action steps that you will take.

9

No Excuses ... We're Doing It!

THE GIRL FROM THE FLOWER SHOP was the first one in our shop that morning. I unloaded my towels from the car and unlocked the back door. I turned on the lights and asked her how she was as I started the coffee pot, needing a cup to recoup from the late night meeting the night before. She didn't seem nearly as enthusiastic as she was before. I was glad to see Dave coming around the corner with his enthusiastic "Good Morning" to keep her on track. She had called everyone she could think of, and nobody was interested. She thought it might be best if she would get her money back.

It didn't take Dave long to distinguish what the problem was. He had a few questions that he had learned from his mentor. What tape have you listened to today? What page did you read of which positive book today? "Well, we don't really listen to tapes," she commented. "I just don't think this is for us," was her final comment. There was no way that Dave was going to let her give up. She was our eighth person, and he was not going to let her fail. He urged her to listen to the tapes called "Getting Started," and he then set a meeting for us to come to their house that next night. He told her to go home, listen to the tapes, and start calling some friends to come over and just check it out.

They lived in a rural area by the river in a single-wide trailer house. Dave got directions on the back of a napkin and put 7:00PM in red. "We'll be there," he promised. We had already set a goal to get to another town, but Dave thought maybe we could do both on the same night. He was obsessed! It was 7:00PM when we pulled in the long country drive, and there was one truck there. As we walked in the house, there were more dried flowers and country crafts on the walls than I was sure the studs of the home could support. Candles were burning, and the lights were dim. I felt like I was in a gift store. We cleared off a table just to allow enough room for their only guests, who were a young couple three years younger than us, to sit and hear the deal. Before we started the young, pregnant wife complained of a migraine and the uncomfortable state of her pregnancy. Her husband, on the other hand, was pretty comfortable as he cracked open a 24-pack, and she positioned her head on the tops of her knees to ease the headache pain. My immediate thought was that we had just entered our worst meeting to date. The hosts for whom we were doing the meeting stood at the kitchen counter and discussed how many said they were coming to the meeting, as if the only sucker yet to come was the dude with the beverages. This was going to be a fun meeting!

Then there was a knock at the door. Another guest arrived. He was a pilot and he farmed. He looked a little older than us and he came dressed in his work clothes from the farm. He stood during the meeting as Dave proceeded to draw circles on a white tablet to demonstrate how our business works since the couple did not have a working VCR to show our video. Dave was nervous. In fact his glass of water was rattling and his head was so close to the tablet I could barely see the circles he was drawing! I'm sure those standing had no idea what the plan was. The meeting lasted less than an hour, and the pregnant woman and her husband left while we made some small talk in the kitchen. Dave walked around the single-wide trailer, and we looked at the photos of the little infant boy who was fast asleep in the nursery. Their dream was to build a new home in the country, and they needed about 1,000 dollars a month. The goal was to never spend another Christmas after this year in the single-wide trailer. We took their dream seriously.

Dave set another meeting on Thursday for those who couldn't make it that night. We didn't have an application yet, but at least we knew we had the hosts committed to one more meeting. Just as we were leaving, the phone rang. It was the young kid. He begged her not to mention that it was him, because he didn't want the pilot to laugh at him for joining. He gave her his credit card over the phone and said to keep it quiet. The funny thing was by the time she got off of the phone the pilot had written his check, and filled out the application to join the business with the executive pack that cost $1,000! He was in the first position before the other application was even filled out. Dave and I continued out the door, as I assured him he was the meeting-man! I couldn't believe the magic he had, and it definitely wasn't in his presentation. I wanted to finish every sentence and correct all of his spelling and his left-handed chicken scratches.

It was about 8:30PM when we left and Dave headed south on a country road toward the next town. Since we were on a roll, we thought, why not drive an hour to where we used to live in Great Bend and show up at our friends' house? When I called them, they urged us not to come that night. Their little boy had a fever and they didn't want us to get whatever he had. Dave said we were already in town and that we wouldn't stay long. We would just drop by with some information. By the time we got to the front door Dave had the cellophane off of the video.

As a mother myself I felt so sorry for the little boy, and wondered if we should stay or come another time. Dave's friend Scott used to be a foreman when they worked on the construction crew together. They reminisced about the old times and Dave let Scott know that it would not be hard to replace his income. It seemed like a lot of people were motivated to quit their jobs, and we were beginning to realize just how many of them did not think they had any other option other than to keep working the very job they hated. We were very enthusiastic about the video and what they were about to see. In fact, we let them know they might not be able to sleep that night from all of the excitement. They laughed as they put the tape in the VCR. We sat on the edge of the couch feeling true excitement as if we were seeing the video for the first time. With every testimony we would become more enthusiastic, and at the end of the video the only question we asked was, "Are you thinking of a few people who might be interested in this?" The reply was usually always the same. Most people could think of a few people. The main excuses people had were that they didn't have the money, or they were worried about having the time. Occasionally, someone might say that they didn't know anyone. Nobody could ever convince us that the fear of failure for them was greater than the odds of success.

With our help, we were sure that everyone we sponsored could get at least four people. Setting a meeting was more important to Dave than getting the application. But I usually wanted their application and credit card so that I knew they were in. The next meeting was set for Friday night. That would allow all of the construction crew to come over. "How about a barbecue and beverages?" Scott asked.

Dave was quick to encourage him to make it simple and not go to a lot of work, because you never knew how many would come. This couple was just sure they could have twenty people, and they were planning to cook for everyone! We worried about their turnout as we left their house, but they filled out the application. We had another person personally sponsored, and that made three applications for the night! I felt flattered, almost as good as the night Dave took his friend Bert with him.

As we drove home, we passed a house that was the home of a couple who had made their fortune in the industry of network marketing. I had heard of their success when I was in my first home-based business, but had never seen their home. This man was very well known in that town. We drove down the driveway and admired the fence, the western flare, and the pool with the slide that wound down in the shadow of the moon. Then we got out of there before anyone would notice we were being so nosy. That was my dream! I wanted to build a home in the country. I had to keep doing the right things long enough, but the vision was becoming clearer and clearer.

We had a chart on the wall at home that showed the goals we had set. With each new meeting we would come home and write in the names of the people we had sponsored, and where they would spill.

There was a cruise coming up around the New Year and all of the top producers in the company with top pin levels were invited. There were several top pin levels, but I was dreaming of at least qualifying to go on what they called The Platinum Club Cruise. We wanted to be in that club and surround ourselves with successful people. We were not sure how many more we needed to sponsor to qualify, but we were sure we would make it because we talked about it every day.

It was late when we got home. Dave's mom kept the babies while we did the meeting. We parked the car close to her front door and got their car seats ready. We ran up to the door to let her know that the couple we sponsored that night in Great Bend spilled onto her top level. It was exciting to know that while she was watching our kids, we were able to help to build her a residual income, and she would soon begin to make some money, too. Everything was starting to come together, and we would soon be receiving monthly checks that were huge! We hugged goodbye and told her we would see her tomorrow. She stopped by the salon each day after she got off of work at the local hospital so she could catch up on all of our progress.

My mom was busy raising four teenagers, but it was so hard for me not to include her in our business. I wanted both of our moms to benefit from all that we were building. It was my twenty-fourth birthday that month in 1996. I had a younger sister whose birthday was a couple of days before me, and my brother in-law Scott had a birthday on the 14th. March was always a fun month of celebrating since Scott was Lori's old flame, and they were pretty close friends. Cindy, Dave's mom, cooked, and we all got together to celebrate. Scott and Lori were turning 21, which was very exciting!

That night I told my mom that I would like to help her get involved in the network-marketing business. She agreed. She said she would buy her products, but there was no way she could sell this thing to anybody. I filled out her application and mailed it off with a check, knowing that our bonus check would soon be in the mail. I didn't want my mom to miss out, and I wanted her to be in before the end of the month. That was my commitment to her, and we started to talk about the possibilities of who we could sponsor.

Uncle Frank was off the list, but we hoped her other brother would join. Heck, he would get involved in anything! We decided to give him a call. It was pretty comical visiting with my uncle and hearing about the next thing he had joined. The company was Destiny, or something of that tone, and it was a phone card company. He was trying to convince Dave and me that we could do both companies, because they wouldn't compete with each other. He said it would help us with our long distance. According to our mentor anything that competed with our time, our energy, our belief, and our finances, other than our company, was not having a definite purpose. This was a training that had been instilled in us just the prior month. We quickly made the decision to get off the phone and move on to another prospect for my mom. Mom was pretty unsure of all of this. She was already worrying about her first month's order, and it was over thirty days away. I guess you could say she had very little faith that things would work to her benefit.

Part of my mother's skepticism must have come from being a single mom with few resources, and she had been taught that hard work was the only way to get ahead. She had calloused hands, would work all day at a factory, and then clean someone's home. After that you might find her feeding livestock or burning wire from the plant so she could sell the iron on the weekend. She was never sitting around. She was always looking for another way to make money for her hard work. I wanted her to see her benefit from work without having to do such manual labor. I had to make this new opportunity work for her.

Dave and I were pretty close to our moms. They were two totally different personalities, but seemed like best friends when we were all together. Nana Cindy would teach my kids to bake cookies and she would rock them in a chair while reading a book or singing a song. While my mom, Nana Lana, would be more likely to have them using the mower at her campground or drive them around town while she was picking up her own small kids. They loved their Nanas, and it never seemed like we were doing much wrong when we left them with Nana to go and do a meeting. We assured our moms that all of their help would soon pay off.

I started to make a list of relatives that I was bound and determined to make successful, even if I had to do it all myself.

Lesson Learned:

> *"Don't worry about the result. Just keep booking the next meeting and stay focused on your dreams and goals."*

<u>10</u>

Think Positively and Believe, No Matter How Hard It Is

IT WAS THE END OF THE MONTH, and we were getting our monthly bills together to see which ones we would be able to pay. The days were very busy with trips to our attorney, running all of the shops, packing up for the weekend, and doing meetings every night of the week. Our house looked like it needed a lot of work. We didn't have curtains, because Dave had begun refinishing the woodwork as my Valentine's surprise. Then he conveniently joined a business the next week that allowed him no time to finish his project. Normal people would have taken a week to fix the mess and get some carpet down on the floor for the babies, but not us. We had pulled up the carpet, stripped the woodwork and there was a tinge of brownish-black liquid running down the walls from the stain that came off of the windows and doorways. The house was built in 1901 and the drafts were bad enough before we took the curtains down.

Chance was learning to walk and had several war wounds to prove that. He loved his spring horse, and he would rock on it for hours in his boots and chaps while I made calls in the evenings. Brooklyn was quite the singer, and she would make it a point to sing as loudly as she could as soon as I got on the phone. If I couldn't get away from them long enough to make a phone call, I would run upstairs and hide in the closet where I quietly called the next person on my list, trying not to make my hiding spot a dead giveaway. I had to be creative with the kids by telling them I was calling Barney or arranging our next trip to the horsey park in order to keep them content while I was on the phone. Sometimes they were flat-out naughty and would hit or bite each other. I would explain to the prospect that I needed to confirm that appointment and then quickly get off the phone. I think it was easier for me having small children than if I had more time to sit and think about the call. I didn't have much time to be scared. I had to take the minute, dial the phone, talk and keep on moving.

I was packing my bag to teach dance and planning to take Brooklyn to dance lessons. She was quite a good little performer at the age of nineteen months and I was just sure she could perform in our recital this May. I couldn't wait for the next day. I had some time with the kids, and Dave was taking the day off from meetings so that he and his brother could catch up at the shop and get our spring crafts ready for the weekend show. We had dozens of wooden bunnies, welcome mats made out of wood for the front door, and lots of furniture and décor. Dave made benches with storage in them and quilt racks and shelves to hold the quilts.

I taught dance until about 7:30PM and then drove up to the hospital to see Cindy. She had a small cyst removed that day, which was a normal procedure for her. She had been dealing with these little lumps since high school, and the doctor she worked with at the hospital said she would have a short surgery and go home the same day. I walked down the hall with my little Brooklyn before picking Chance up from day care, and Dave and Scott were standing outside of the hospital room. The news was not good. It was breast cancer. I had flashbacks of all of the people I loved who I had lost to this horrible disease. There is nothing any worse that could happen. I was not sure I could handle many more of His tests. I was very close to my mother-in-law, and she was the Nana of my babies. She was so young. We stood in the hall and cried. Cindy was not awake yet. The boys were in a discussion with her doctor listening to her options and they were planning to get her to a specialist as soon as possible. The doctor said it could take several weeks to get an appointment with a good doctor. I immediately left the hospital, picked up Chance, and called my mother. I couldn't handle the news. The boys seemed to be very scared, and I didn't want to add to their fear with my experiences from the past and all of my loved ones I'd lost to cancer. Mom encouraged me to call my uncle Frank. She believed that with his powerful connections and the people he knew in Wichita, we could get Cindy the best doctor there was. Frank golfed with an oncologist at the private country club golf course where they lived. Mom was on the phone calling him before I left her house. I encouraged her to let

Cindy work through this first and we would talk to my uncle later in the week. My mom decided not to waste any time. We were all worried about Cindy.

Dave believed everything would work out, and he was optimistic that they had it under control and that nothing would take her from us. I knew he was scared, but men cannot show their emotions like women can or they would feel like they are not masculine or something. He was keeping us all together and the next day the doctor advised Cindy that it could be six weeks before she could get in to see the specialist. That night we placed a call to Uncle Frank. Within a few days Cindy was in the hands of the greatest surgeon in Wichita.

There was a schedule of surgeries, treatments, and doctor appointments that was pretty urgent. Dave and I agreed we needed to be there with her, and we would get through this as a family. It was good to be self-employed, because it allowed us to set our own schedules. We were sure that the lady who helped us out at the store would take good care of our business, as the spring season would be picking up soon.

I had some bookwork to do because the consigners were coming in this week to pick up paychecks from their inventory we had sold in the store. I was anxious to see what their paychecks would be and to confirm that I could cover all of our store expenses. I added the inventory slips of items sold and it seemed as though we had a pretty good month. I wrote the checks to the people who had left their items in the store and had their unsold items ready for them to pick up. It was always nice to see them come in and pick up their checks, as they brought new inventory for the following month.

One particular vendor was very proud of her flower arrangements. She was in the network marketing business with us and was actually doing quite well. She was on our seventh or eighth level under that famous couple from the trailer house. The pilot had sponsored a couple from Quinter, Kansas who had over ten personally sponsored people. The lady with the flowers was under them. She loved our nutritional products and she loved our store. As she walked around the store she noticed that some of her items were missing, but they weren't listed on the sheet listing items sold and that I had just paid her for. There was no way that this could be a mistake on our part, because we had a ticket book for sales and a file drawer for each tag that was removed as it was sold. All of the tickets from the drawer went in the envelopes with the commission checks. I told her I would look into it, and I assured her we would make it right with her. Some of her arrangements sold for forty dollars and others were over a hundred dollars.

It was a long day at the shop, and I had a lot of cleaning to do. I emptied the trash and cleaned the coffee pots in the coffee bar. I loaded all of the soiled towels from the salon into my car and cleaned the bathrooms getting ready for a busy day tomorrow. There was sawdust tracked from the back of the shop to the front doors from all of the times Dave had to come out and make lattes and mochas while I was tending the clients in the salon. Dave was a young, nice looking man, and I was just sure that some of the girls came in just to have him make them a coffee. I would beat on his door if I could not walk away from my salon so he could come out to fix the coffee orders or sell crafts and furniture. The building was big enough to house all five businesses, and dividers of lattice separated the departments so it was easy for me to watch the shoppers. I was sure there was no way that a flower arrangement could walk out that door without my seeing it.

As I hauled the trash out to the dumpster I noticed several tags in the bottom of the trash bag. I was confused. Why would anyone tear off a price tag and put it in the trash instead of placing it in the consignment drawer? Would an employee take cash out of the drawer and hide the tag? How many items had this happened with? I added the amounts from the tags and found that many of them were the nicer missing flower arrangements. The total cost for the day of items lost came to $74.00. If we were losing that kind of money each day, we couldn't afford to have employees. Dave and I made a decision to fire the girl we hired to work in the store and replace her with a close friend or family member we could trust. How would I confront this girl? She was a friend and I thought she was honest. She bought me nice gifts and pretended to be looking out for my best interests. I couldn't believe someone would steal from the store!

I had ordered a tape set by Jim Rohn called "The Art of Exceptional Living." If there was an art to it, I needed to learn it. I wasn't in the mood for a business tape and I didn't want to call anyone to set up a meeting. I cleaned up the kitchen and rocked the kids to sleep listening to Jim Rohn. He had a very monotone voice, which wasn't my usual choice of speaker, but I liked the information. At first he didn't make me feel better, and he was not very motivating. But the story on the first tape happened to be about a business partner of his that cheated him out of over a half of a million dollars. I realized he was laughing about it! Soon he encouraged me to laugh, since the lesson was that I would grow from this and some day it would make a good story. His final words of encouragement were to make me glad that I learned it losing a small amount (such as $74.00 a day), instead of $4,000 a day which I would soon be making. If it wasn't for the tape I might have wanted to write the girl from our shop a death threat, but instead the tape made me feel a little bit better. Could this be why we were falling behind, because we were paying for goods that were walking out the door? Could this be part of the reason the store wasn't profitable, no matter how much we advertised or how hard we worked? It seemed to be the month of adversity at the Pitcock's house. Without the tapes, I was sure I would be on the verge of a nervous breakdown.

It is easy to give up and quit when times get tough and when there seems to be no point in working. Each day it was harder and harder to get excited about the shop, the studio, the salon, and the business, because there was never enough money left for us. We were not quitters and we worked harder than anyone I could think of to compare ourselves to. Dave and I made a commitment to find a way to build this business so big that it would replace our income so we could be at home with family doing what we wanted, when we wanted, and having the money to pay for it. Soon every day would be a Saturday, and people would drive by the park and see us pushing our kids on the swings on a Tuesday afternoon. That would really have the town talking … and we couldn't wait for that day.

The people at the hospital were starting to sign up under Cindy, the people on Main Street were joining under many of the business people in town, and it was time for us to start some new groups in other towns. I decided to ride with Dave to Colby, Kansas to meet the group out there that was building to be so big. The couple in the trailer still only had two personals, but their group had over eighty in it by the end of the month. The company paid an average of 10% on all of the people in your organization and the product orders they had placed. The residual checks were monthly paychecks based on that 10% average of all of the product volume ordered. This check would continue to come in, even if you stopped working because of the fact that everyone ordered each month in order to stay active. With 100 people placing orders they could earn 1,000 a month! Their earnings from their residual check would be near a thousand dollars in no time. I was so happy for them. They would be able to afford that house in the country that was their dream. Colby was the town where

Dave had gone to college and got involved in rodeo. He had a full-ride baseball scholarship to attend college, but fell in love with bull riding instead. He had given up his baseball scholarship and joined the college rodeo team.

We drove around, looked at his old apartment, and joked about old girlfriends and college memories he had. We pulled into a restaurant to get a quick buffet and decided to call an old friend from high school who was attending Wichita State University. She was my friend, but she had also been very close to Dave. He made the call to see if she was interested in coming to our meeting. It seemed so much fun for us to be getting ready for a huge meeting by calling people together from our list instead of our being in separate towns. But I was glad I was in the car with Dave when he called her. I've never seen anyone hurt his feelings so badly. Not only did she let him know she had no interest, but she accused him of being a scam artist and told him people in Wichita go to jail for junk like this! I wasn't sure he would recuperate, let alone be able to do a meeting in an hour. I felt so sorry for Dave, and I knew exactly how he felt. This had happened to me several times during that first month, but nobody had nailed Dave with this type of negativity until that night. I comforted him by saying that she would always be that way, and her opinion wasn't going to affect our success in this business. Sometimes this is easier said than believed, but it was true. I just remembered what our mentor's assistant taught us that day on the phone:

"You can either take advice from someone making thirty thousand a year, or you can take advice from someone making thirty thousand a month. It's your decision about who you want to trust."

I learned that sometimes free advice is worth just what it costs.

There were about sixty people at the community center waiting to see the plan, and Dave was about to get sick. He had no idea how he was going to do this meeting; he was wondering if his old friend was right. We tried to pump each other up, wishing we had time to listen to our favorite tape, but we decided to use a phrase from the training system, "Fake it until you make it." That's exactly what we did. We got up there and told the story with pure enthusiasm and vision of where we were headed. That night we went home with a half a dozen applications and many more who attended were headed home to fax in their information. There was no longer a question that one person's opinion of us was going to affect our success. The drive home gave us some time to visit and we talked about our dreams and how our life would be by Christmas. We had our planners out booking more meetings, and we listened to tapes as we drove.

Three hours is about a three-tape drive, and that is pretty much how we measured our trips to do meetings. It was nothing to drive to Kansas City and back in an evening. In fact, we could listen to an entire album during that trip. Our vehicle became our University on Wheels. The speaker on the tape said if you listen to a thousand tapes, you will be financially free; and we were well on our way to that destination. The Chris LeDoux tapes were taking a back seat in our tape case. Although we thought we would miss listening to music, the personal development tapes were really easy to listen to and they paid a lot better. There was always time for one or two of our favorite songs after our brains were completely full of information and on overload.

There was a convention coming, and on the audio tapes the top leaders were promoting the event. I had no idea how we could possibly afford to get to Chicago, Illinois. The tickets were several hundred dollars each, but I was sure wishing we could be there. Dave and I were trying to think of creative ways that we could afford to go. Although we had close to a hundred people that we knew of in our downline, we hadn't received our check for the second month. I wondered how much our check would be. We had sponsored four people for the month of March and many others who joined under our friends. We were anxious to see what our check would be. Regardless of the size of the check, we wanted to be able to go to Chicago.

I wrote an ad for a garage sale, and we made a list of everything we could do without if selling them meant we could attend this big event and meet all of the top leaders we had been listening to on the tapes. I could sell some of my crafty stuff and I was sure that Dave could sell all of his tools and fishing equipment. I told him he could buy all new when summer came because we would soon be rich! I believed that with all of my heart!

Our sponsor happened to be in town for the day and I told him of our desire to go to the big event. He offered to buy my double china hutch that held all of my dishes and wedding stuff. This would be enough money for one of the tickets. He had a buyer for the hutch on his route, and he could not get one ordered in time for the delivery. It was tough, but I did it. I unloaded the stuff and neatly placed it in tissue paper in a box labeled "china hutch," and we had enough money for one of the $300.00 tickets. Our garage sale was scheduled for Saturday, and I worked through the middle of the night to round up enough stuff to make it look full. None of the stuff was anything I couldn't replace, but a lot of it was much nicer than your normal garage sale items.

There was no question when the man interested in the five hundred dollar table-saw offered me $250.00 cash; I promptly asked him if he needed help loading it. We were on our way to Chicago and had four months to hit our goal of sponsoring ten people and helping each one sponsor at least one. We had to sponsor ten people and help each of them enroll at least one friend in the business in order to be qualified as Platinum. We had to do this by May and hold that rank for three months, or we would not be recognized on stage at the awards ceremony. If we could hit it, we would get to shake the president's hand, and we would have our name read and be called on stage during the recognition ceremony and parade of platinums. Most company members strive for this to have the recognition of being in the elite circle of leaders and mentors. We had a way to go, but I knew we could help enough people in order for us to reach this level of recognition. If we could do it, we could also buy a ticket to go on the Leadership Cruise!

We were on a mission, in spite of all of the adversity that seemed to be raining on us from a slow moving cloud. According to the books we were reading and the tapes we were listening to, it wasn't what was happening to us that would matter. It's what we did about it that would make the difference. Sometimes we didn't know what to do, but ACTION CURES FEAR continued to be our motto.

Dave at a college rodeo in 1989

Dave and I pose with our parents on our wedding day. Although they were divorced at the time, this is the only photo I have with my mom and dad.

Newlyweds Barb and Dave Pitcock with Dave's brother Scott, his best man in our wedding.

Humble beginnings: The trailer and my shop that we moved several times during those first few years we were married.

Dave getting ready to get on the bull in the chute at Garden City.

Our little cabin in Cody, Wyoming. This is the cabin where we began our journey as a couple.

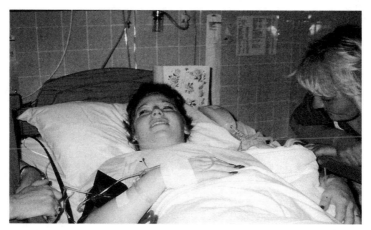

In this photo I am in ICU with my blood pressure at 240 over 120, which caused my ear drums to burst. Toxemia HELLPS Syndrome and toxic poisoning caused my liver to shut down.

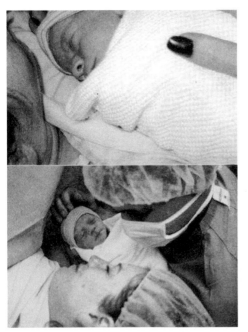

Miracle baby Brooklyn Nicole, the greatest accomplishment of my life happened the day I became a mom. If there is one thing I desire to be in life, it is to be the best mom on the planet! She literally would fit in your hand. It was such a miracle to see her little hands and feet and to know that she was going to be okay.

Dave and I are with our sponsor, Bert Leach, at our first meeting together in direct sales as a couple. Our team t-shirts read, "Believe it and Achieve it ... Doubt it and Go without it!"

Three babies in four years: Chance David, Brooklyn Nicole, and Kali Anne

Our family in the fall of 1998

The Q 45 Infinity that we dreamed of at the convention became a reality within 90 days. This is our photo driving it off the lot car seats and all! The car cost more than our first home!

Presidential Platinums, David and Barb Pitcock, 2001. Here VP Jana Mitcham and President David Bertrand congratulate Dave and me. At the far right is Green Bay Packers legend, Jerry Kramer. We had reached the top and were the #1 producer at the age of 28 years old.

Our story was *featured* on the cover of Lifestyles Magazine *three times.*
This one was in 1999 as 5-Star Platinums.

This photo is our family today, taken in 2009 at Christmas in our home. Left to right: Brooklyn, Kali Anne, Dave, Barb, and Chance

Barb Pitcock, senior year, 1989

This photo was taken in February of 2001. The cruise we took included my parents, Dave's mom, and all of my siblings. This was just months after the loss of Dave's younger brother Scott, so at Christmas we filled the stockings with free cruise tickets. We made a decision to focus on what was most important and spend time with the people we love. Front row: Dave's mom Cindy is holding Chance, my younger sister Traci is holding Brooklyn, I am holding Kali Anne, and my mother is to my left.

The back row includes my sister Lori, her husband Duke, my younger brothers Jeremy and Mark, and my husband Dave.

11

I'd Rather Try and Fail Than Never Try

THE SMELL OF "HOME SWEET HOME" was more than my favorite flavor of candle. It was the aroma that said, "You have a day off and you get to play with your kids." It was Easter and our businesses were closed. Apparently, no one had a meeting we needed to do. The kids were anticipating a busy day with Easter baskets, church, and lots of aunts and uncles. I don't know if the kids were anticipating anything, but being the festive mom that I was, I was sure that they were excited for the big day. I drove up to our gift shop to take home some of my favorite flavored coffees and party dips so Dave and I could have a cup of coffee together and get ready for Easter dinner with family. It was pretty ironic to think that we owned a craft store and a coffee bar, but yet we seldom had time to enjoy a quiet cup of coffee that we promoted or a chance to spread the holiday crafts in our own home. The store I always dreamed of was a year-round-Christmas store, and now that I had achieved the dream of opening the store, I seldom had the chance to decorate my own home. I grabbed a wooden Easter bunny to set outside our front door to surprise the kids and headed back home with several gifts for Dave's little cousins who would be at his grandma's house later.

On my way home I passed that little First Baptist Church where I had grown up and where my grandma took me each Sunday. Now that I was a grown woman, the choice of where to go on Sunday was getting tougher and tougher. Dave was raised a Lutheran, but we hadn't gone there much together. Right behind the Lutheran Church was a lot that was shared by the First Baptist Church. The challenge with going to the First Baptist Church was that we would be the only couple under the age of seventy, and since there was no nursery for the kids that made it tough to get anything out of the sermon. I wanted to go to church with my children and my husband, but we could not find a church in our small town with the enthusiasm we experienced both in Wyoming and in the church where we were married in Great Bend. Finding a church like the one we were married in, with a live band and a young energetic leader was unusual, but since it was about an hour's drive to Great Bend, we opted to go to the Lutheran Church. It was a also great church, but it just never felt like home to me. I guess it's all in how I was raised.

Everyone has their own idea of religion and their own opinion on what you need to do and how you need to get there. Dave and I were in agreement that attending church built our faith and gave us a place to worship, and we weren't going to argue over who was right and who was wrong. My faith was stronger than ever, and I wished there was somewhere I could go to get the music, sermons, and friendships I had experienced in the other towns where we had lived. I hadn't realized how fortunate we were when we lived where we had a church family and a place that we felt welcome. Dave assured me that it was about my relationship with God and not my attendance record. There are a lot of people that go to church each week, but yet they don't have faith or love in their hearts. Dave was always helping me grow spiritually. I was raised feeling guilty if I didn't attend church every Sunday. I had to admit I had never experienced such faith and so many miracles, and all I had to do was pray and have belief. God was definitely working in my life.

It was so much fun to have a day at home and be able to do all the things I had wanted. Each night as I drove to a meeting or the mornings when I headed to work, I would dream of having a day to myself. Easter break included Monday, and I had big plans for the long weekend.

As we enjoyed our cup of coffee together, we visited about the upcoming month and all that we had accomplished in March. It was time to build and we knew that the month ahead was going to be our best month ever. There was a message on our answering machine from the top money earner in the company. This was the guy who we listened to on every training tape. It was really him! He didn't have his assistant call. He actually called, said he couldn't wait to meet us, and informed us he had booked a meeting to do a presentation in our home town! He was a little off on the name of our home town. He had actually booked the meeting about thirty miles from us in Hays, Kansas. I realized he had chosen a town with an airport to land his private jet. We were so excited!

We immediately set a goal to have the meeting room full of new people. I went from wanting to rest to wondering who I could call on Easter. Together we strategized our goals, our deadlines, and the commitments we would make together. We made plans to move a part-time nanny into our basement and give her free room and board for taking care of the children. The girl we had in mind would be attending Fort Hays State University the following semester and was a family friend. We had to get creative with our financial situation and our tending to the children while we built the business.

I sat on the front porch that incredible afternoon and dreamed of the way our lives would someday be. It was great to see the purple hyacinths blooming and think of putting some fresh pots by the front door. It was time to change the out-dated winter wreath to something that said spring and summer. I loved to decorate. In fact, I would change my yard and door for every season, but lately it seemed like there wasn't much time for what I loved to do. Dave would talk about going to play golf with a friend or going to fish at the river, but then he would remind me of our commitments. We would both agree we could do whatever we wanted once we helped enough other people get what they wanted. Our focus was finding four other people who had the desire to get to the leadership level we were. 4-Star was our goal, which was the true freedom level. People at this level were making six–figure incomes, driving free cars and financially free! We weren't there yet, but we talked like we were!

Sometimes we sat and talked about the way it feels to be a 4-star and the freedom we would soon have as if it had already happened. We couldn't afford to talk about the past or where we were in our current difficult situation. Our entire focus was on the positive affirmations. It felt sometimes as if we had already reached our goal.

Our babies were so close in age that it was easier to sleep with both of them than it was to get up and feed two at separate times of the night. We would often spend our early mornings playing with them before we got up to head off to work. Dave would talk as if we were retired, and he would give orders to our full-time maid to get the kids' breakfast ready and start the coffee for us. Then we would giggle and say, "She's not listening, is she?" We would even call her name out loud, and then laugh at the fact that she was our imaginary friend. We knew that it wouldn't be long before someone else would be doing some of the housework and helping with laundry. That was definitely on my dream board, because at the rate these babies were growing, playing with them was so much more important than all of cleaning that needed to be done.

Easter came and went, and it was fun to dress up the kids and go visit grandmas and great-grandmas. I always wished my dad could see how beautiful these little kids were as we left Dave's dad's house. It was fun to show them off. It seemed like they could do no wrong in our eyes, but yet they were into everything. I couldn't wait until I could afford to go shopping to buy them new outfits or cute little toys instead of the hand-me-downs or used clothing I would get at Once Upon a Child. I loved to go there and look for name-brand used clothes, but it would be fun to get them the right sizes and something to match occasionally.

It was getting harder and harder to leave the kids each morning. I had a recipe box full of index cards with people's accounts who owed money for haircuts, hair spray, and perms. It was hard to believe that a family would schedule haircuts and colors for their kids or spouse and tell me to put it on a bill. There was almost a thousand dollars in accounts receivables for $7.00 haircuts. I had a list of people to send bills to and my mother-in-law had offered to help me call to collect from them. I had a busy week on the books, but I could see that many of them were non-paying customers. There was a family that came in every week or two to receive services in-trade for my paying off my wedding dress, which the mother had sewn by hand. Had I known I would have to cut their hair for four years to pay it off I might have borrowed one. When she offered to sew the dress for me, I assumed it would be much more affordable than the one I dreamed of purchasing. So, I agreed. But my dress was beautiful, and I was reminded of this each week when the family came for products, services, coffee, and sometimes even gifts from the store.

Dave and I had never had anyone give us a handout and we were definitely working as hard as we could. We didn't grow up with money, but our parents had taught us to work hard. We were finding ourselves working harder and harder with less and less time together. We were leaving our kids early each morning and picking them up at dark.

It was getting monotonous to work so hard and take home so little, but I could do it for a while longer, thinking soon we would be free! The week went by fast and on Friday Dave and I took off to see our attorney. He was very intimidating and most people believed he was the best attorney in the area. I trusted him and I hoped they were right. I was a bit emotional about the lawsuit as we told him our intentions and how we felt that we had done nothing wrong. He listened and he, too, said it was a peculiar case, and didn't understand the claim for damages from our decision to order T-shirts from a new company.

He agreed to represent us in this case, and as he looked over our situation he had a puzzled look on his face. He asked what was keeping us from bankruptcy. He urged us to file Chapter 11 to protect our personal property and any assets. He said that way we would not have to worry if we lost this lawsuit and were required to pay the fifty thousand to the guy who we offended by shopping out of town. I guess you could say it was the final straw for me. I blamed other people and was full of anger that I was in this situation. "Why us?" I asked him. "Why would anyone want to sue us? We are good honest people just trying to be creative and make a living to support our family." I just wanted to pay my bills and have a little bit extra. I wanted to protect my family, and I wished that the lawsuit would just go away.

We had to list our assets and any equity we had. We had worked so hard to put the down payment on the house we were leasing. We had finally saved up enough money to leave a rental house and had put fifteen thousand dollars down on the house in order to have the purchase option. That fifteen thousand represented a lot of $7.00 haircuts and many $10.00 craft sales. Our monthly payments were going towards the purchase price and it would take years to completely pay for the house. The value of the home had increased substantially and we had to list that on the sheet. I was scared, and I felt like a criminal. There was no way we could risk losing all that we had worked for, could we?

Our attorney suggested that just one of us file bankruptcy in order to take this lawsuit off the books. I would continue to pay everything off and not include my name with Dave's Chapter 11 filing. We didn't realize at that time what all of these legal documents meant and what it would do to our credit. At the time, we were young, scared and it sounded like no big deal. We would continue to pay for our cars and keep them and continue to pay for our home and keep it. As I understood, filing bankruptcy would be to relieve us from the pressure of the lawsuit that was filed as the Shirt Company vs. David Pitcock. For a $750.00 filing fee we would be out from under the pressure of the constant depositions and arguing who was right or wrong between our attorneys. We were twenty-four years old and had no idea this would be one of the biggest decisions we would ever make. We had to list everything we owned and all of our debts. Of course, we had about ten thousand dollars worth of campaign souvenirs and merchandise in our basement that we would never try to sell again, but that was something we agreed was a hard lesson learned. Dave suggested that we keep the T-shirts until they were antiques, and maybe someday they would be worth something again. That was a great idea, but the money would have been good then, not later.

It was a tough decision for two young kids that had no idea what they were doing, but we both agreed we would not include any of our local bills, our house, or our vehicles in the filing. Our goal was to pay off everyone, because we believed our ship was coming in soon. It did feel like it was coming in, just not fast enough to fend off the wolves.

To drive to the city, park in a parking garage, and meet a new attorney with our papers to file our bankruptcy was one of the scariest things I think we ever went through. Dave didn't say much but we did what we were urged to do. That day changed my husband for a very long time. The shame that came with the title of that Chapter 11 was harder for him than if we had lost our home to the guy who claimed we owed him damages for the T-shirts we bought out of town.

Honestly, looking back, if we had known how quickly things could turn around for us, we would have never agreed to file. Because we were in our early twenties we were very young to achieve the kind of success we had experienced. Success was happening faster than our own self-esteem or any personal growth could quite keep up with it. Many of our friends were working from nine to five for a weekly paycheck with no risk, and no chance of failing; however, they were broker than broke. I wanted more for my family, and I had big dreams and goals. We had worked hard and our businesses did very well, but there were a lot of other variables that came into play than just our ability to work hard. I could blame the lawsuit, the employee, or the small town where only some townspeople shopped as many others drove thirty miles away to buy their gifts. I could blame the economy, or Dave and I could blame each other for business decisions we made in the store and the salon. Mostly we just blamed ourselves. We felt like failures, and we were ashamed of our decisions. Together we had big dreams in a small town, and many of the people in our town we were trying to set on fire were excited to stomp out the flames as fast as we could light them. There were a lot of dream stealers in our town.

The books we read helped a lot, as they told us that it was better to have tried and failed than to have never tried at all. Walt Disney's story of filing bankruptcy seven times made us feel not quite like such losers, but it didn't fix it. Nothing I could say would make Dave feel any better about our decision. The positive thing for me was that I knew I was going to be able to pay the people the money I owed. It was hard to live in a small town where there was so much talk and gossip. For Dave, it was more than just emotional. His pride suffered, and he just wanted to hide his face and leave our home town. It was hard for him to even go to work anymore. He didn't feel an ounce of pride or accomplishment from any of our endeavors.

We would second guess our decision and talk about what we should have done differently on a daily basis. According to our attorney we could have been in this lawsuit for a long time. The attorney fees alone were more than our monthly income. The filing was the only answer to the T-shirt hearings and we were ready for it all to end.

We filed our bankruptcy in a city pretty far from home. I was sure it wouldn't be in our local paper. As long as I would pay all of our bills and continue on as if it didn't happen, maybe time would ease our embarrassment and the feeling of being a financial failure. I didn't even tell my own mother and I was sure that Dave wouldn't tell anyone either. It was a relief to think that I wouldn't have to spend another day in a courtroom giving a deposition to an attorney questioning me about some stupid T-shirts while I asked to be excused to nurse my baby.

I guess it never dawned on me that some people are so bored that they spend their time going through papers reading the obituaries, the weddings, and the bankruptcies; but believe it or not, there are people who don't have anything more exciting to do. Even before having children and five businesses to run, I can honestly say I didn't find any entertainment in those sections of the newspaper. I always wanted others to succeed and was happy for them. I had enough goals and objectives on my own daily list that taking time to check out everyone else's business would not have fit into my daily routine. I am thankful for that, and I pray for the people who are in a rut of gossip and negative news that someday they have a dream big enough to capture their attention in a way it consumes them like I was consumed.

I'm sure you can guess what the outcome of this story is. It only took one person to read the Wichita newspaper, and we might as well have held a press conference on the courthouse lawn. My mother called me in shock, as she had no idea we were experiencing so many challenges. I hadn't thought about one of Cindy's sisters living just outside of Wichita, plus I didn't think they would have any interest in that part of the news. By this time our downline had grown to over two hundred people and they thought that after three months of our joining a home based business, we must be over-night millionaires. The thought of us having any financial challenges created doubt, and that was enough to make many of the people in our business resign from the program immediately. Our phone started to ring. It wasn't easy, but we were honest about the situation. We assured our friends and family this was a business decision based on an issue totally outside of our home based business. No matter what we told people, it didn't take away the pain, the embarrassment, or the feeling of being a bad person. We regretted our decision every day.

Many times people in your home town want you to do well, but just not too well. Now, I am speaking in generalities. I know there are some kind people in each town, but I also know there that are people who are jealous of anyone who succeeds and gets ahead of them. When we were broke, everyone loved us and supported us and our businesses. However, once we started to make some good money and find a way out of the forty-year rut (working for forty years to retire and live on half of what you already couldn't afford to live on), people questioned our decisions and our business venture. I could tell there was a difference in the number of people shopping in the gift store. Perhaps the rumors had people scared to come inside and see for themselves if we were still there or not. Many people ridiculed us and called us crooks, saying that we had taken advantage of people and didn't pay our bills. This was devastating, and it was too late to turn back the poor decisions we had made.

We knew that we could either make excuses, or we could make money—we couldn't do both. Dave and I had every reason to give up, but we wouldn't do it. We just kept dreaming of the day that our financial worries would all be behind us, and we prayed that day would come soon. I prayed for forgiveness and that I would be led in the right direction to do what I was supposed to do with the talents and the gifts with which I had been blessed. I was confused and wondered why this was all happening to us.

I searched for wisdom in the personal development books and in the Bible. I looked for the answers and prayed for it to all go away, but it didn't. I would write in my journal and try to get the fear out of my mind before I laid down each night. I was trying to grow as a person during this time of adversity. I wanted to be successful, and I knew I wasn't a failure.

Lesson Learned:

"Take responsibility for your past, and don't blame others for your failures. Learn from your mistakes and don't make the same mistakes again. If you accept defeat and don't take action, you have failed. If you learn from your mistakes and become a stronger person, you will grow. Yesterday is gone and you can't change it, but tomorrow is yours to create."

BARB PITCOCK

12

A Breakdown, or a Breakthrough— It's Your Decision

DAVE AND I ENTERED IN A LOT OF LARGE CRAFT SHOWS and focused on selling the big ticket items, mainly our solid oak reproduction furniture. Selling one or two pieces of furniture easily made up for over a hundred of our little fresh scented candles. Maybe this was God's way of telling us there was something bigger in store for us.

Mother's Day was always a busy weekend for us. We decided to put our entire inventory outside on the front walk with "SALE" banners and displays. We had a great weekend, and the inventory was flying out the door. I hated to pay to re-order anything because it was so nice to be able to have money to pay off the vendors we owed. That is exactly what we did. Without restocking the smaller items where our shelves were getting bare, we packed in the solid oak furniture. Our sponsor Bert came through town with a full trailer of furniture once a month and he left us fully stocked.

That night we invited our moms to dinner for Mother's Day. Chance was in his little tub floating in the big tub and Brooklyn was close by dumping buckets of water over his little head. They loved their baths, and many times Daddy would even come in and tease them or video them playing in the water. This particular Mother's Day was one I will never forget. I had not only one, but two little babies by my second Mother's Day. I felt extremely blessed, because we not only had two beautiful, healthy children. We ourselves had two amazing moms.

Dave's mom paid us with an early visit, and I could tell when she walked into my bathroom it wasn't just to see the kids. Her first chemotherapy treatment had gone pretty well, but today she was starting to lose her hair. She was prepared for this, or she thought she was. Of course, when it happened, it was such an emotional time for both of us. Trying to be positive about the situation, we both cried and laughed as we combed it out and the kids sat in the tub watching us. I had fixed her a wig that was short, spunky and looked so much like her natural hair we knew nobody would notice. I enjoyed making people look better and feel better. It was all I could do to keep from crying, but I was determined to make her look beautiful. It wasn't hard to do, but it seemed so unfair that something like this would happen on Mother's Day to a woman who was so dear to us. We were confident that her hair would grow back soon, and she would be well. She was determined to beat this battle and live a long happy life watching her grandchildren grow up.

That night my problems seemed pretty minor. I had my health, and that was a lot more important than any material thing or any bill I had worried about all month. Perhaps that was the lesson I needed to learn. I never felt sorry for myself again. I just pressed on, and in spite of anyone else's opinion, I knew I was forgiven for my sins. I was working every day to become a better person and do more with the talents God had blessed me with. It wasn't easy, because one moment I think that way and the next moment I thought maybe I was just being brainwashed by positive thinkers. I did have to admit, though, it was easier when I was around the positive people than when I was with the negative people.

When you think your problems are big, just rest assured there is always someone out there who would trade places with you. As I put myself in Cindy's shoes, I imagined her feelings as she sat in a room of people having a conversation about their sore throats. The smallest little sniffle had them complaining. I felt guilty mentioning that I was tired or that my back was sore because I had just carried two children around all day long. Every day that we are alive is a blessing. There is nothing that is so big that God cannot take care of it. The challenge is having faith and believing that there is hope that you can overcome the problems that you face. It takes more than just praying for something to happen. It takes having faith that it will come to fruition and taking action as if it already has. I once listened to a sermon where the preacher was talking about God meeting us at our level of expectancy. If we expect things to be good, they will be ... and if we doubt, it is hard for us to attract the things we want. Visualizing the outcome in your mind is one of the most powerful things I have ever experienced. Try it for yourself, and you will find that if you hold the thought in your mind on a regular basis and you do this long enough ... your subconscious mind does not know the difference between what is real and what is imagined.

I had to change my beliefs. Although during my childhood I lost everyone I ever loved who was diagnosed with cancer, this time the outcome was different. There are some things we cannot change. But miracles do happen every single day to those who have faith and believe. Cindy was optimistic and we dreamed of the day she would be well. I had fear, and I kept reflecting back and wondering why things had happened in my past. Maybe Cindy could get well, but I didn't understand why that couldn't have happened for my Grandma Mills. My grandma had raised me during my early childhood and she was everything to me. She fought so hard to live and she had an extreme faith. When she lost her battle with cancer, after years of praying and believing she would be healed, I was angry. It didn't make any sense to me. Realizing that I do not know all of the answers, it is sometimes hard for me to teach others to have faith when life isn't always fair, and many times it doesn't make sense.

In the grand scheme of things, I believe that our life here is very short. In fact, it has been called a blink of an eye in time compared to eternity. I am not the expert on why life is not fair. I do believe that there is a purpose for each of us in this life, and we have a short time here to make a difference. My grandma and grandpa definitely lived lives of greatness, and they changed more lives than I could ever dream of touching. Life is not always about how long we live, but how we truly live during the time we have here. I encourage people to realize that life is short. Don't wait to do things that you dream of, because there is no guarantee how long any of us will have. The lessons during these months just reaffirmed to me that there was no reason to build our business slowly and take our time. We had to stay focused and experience freedom from stress. We had to break free from the bondage of debts and worries. We had to make the most of every day we had with the people we loved, because there were no guarantees.

The end of May was fast approaching, and in order for us to hit our goal, we had to reach it by the last day of May. We had to be qualified by this date in order to be recognized at our company's convention. We had every reason in the world to say it wasn't going to happen this month, but our goal all along had been to hit the next pin level. We had sponsored about fifteen friends into the business, but of those, only about half of them had sponsored someone. In order to qualify for the next pin level, we had to have been fully qualified for the previous pin level the month before. Part of qualifying was purchasing more than the minimum in products.

When I called to check on how many active people we needed to have to get to our goal of the Platinum level, I was told that I missed the commissions because I had not ordered enough products to meet the volume requirement for this.

Some people liked to sell, and others chose to order just what they needed for themselves. The only requirement was that you move at least 100 in products for the month. Since the products could be used for personal consumption and I was never very good at selling products I was more likely to give them away. Suddenly I found out that we didn't make it because I hadn't ordered enough! We weren't even qualified for the Gold level, because I had chosen to save sixty dollars by ordering the minimum amount of products. I hadn't thought it was worth it to order the extra products that second month because our group was pretty small. It didn't seem logical to spend that much money on products I might not use. But our commissions would have been more than three times what I spent, if I had just placed the order for the extra amount.

As a new leader in the company, I had a lot of lessons to learn. I was new to the business and nickel and diming was the kind of decision I made.

I was so focused on what I was spending I hadn't learned that if I used them as samples it would help me build my downline and get others started on the products.

My upline had told me to order more than the minimum amount, but I was still in my hard-headed state, thinking everyone was trying to benefit from my purchase. Within thirty days I developed leadership thinking and never again questioned ordering more than the minimum amount.

At this point, not only did I need three people to sponsor one person, I needed to order $300.00 of products to reach the next pin level. I couldn't imagine that happening with just a few days left. I started to call some of our personals to try to motivate them to do something, but it took so much out of me. My energy was less after the calls than if I had given them someone I sponsored. The tapes said not to give people away, but I had to hit this pin level. I was on the phone in hot pursuit of some new people.

I got out our phone book and started to call Shawn, one of Dave's old college friends from Burwell, Nebraska. I was nervous like I had never been and just as he answered, I hung up. I couldn't do it. I was missing that fire I used to have on the phone. I felt like the phone was harder to pick up than it was the first day I had started the business. What was wrong with me?

Brooklyn and Chance needed my attention, so I played with them a while. Then I plugged in a movie so they would be entertained while I made some calls. I sat in the chair rocking Chance to sleep as I listened to Brooklyn quietly playing in the other room. I laughed as I listened to her talk to herself, and thought to myself, what a character she is talking to her imaginary friend. She was telling him all about her daddy, her mommy, her Bubby, and the kitty named Alice. She was quite the talker. In fact, as a one-year-old, she would carry on an entire conversation. She came around the corner with the phone and said, "Mommy, it is for you!" I didn't even hear the phone ring. It was Shawn, Dave's friend from Nebraska. I was in shock, because I had dialed him earlier and I had hung up the phone when he answered! He asked me how Brooklyn got his number to dial it. I acted totally confused as if she must have hit speed dial, and he was in the memory of our saved numbers. I am sure he knew I was lying. I was too embarrassed to admit that I had called and hung up, and then Brooklyn had hit the redial button.

Shawn asked about Dave, the kids, and rodeo. We reminisced about their days at Colby Community College, as if I hadn't heard those rodeo stories at least twenty times, and I laughed like I was entertained and had never heard the stories before. He was a nice guy, and asked me to have Dave call about a new business venture he was looking at and wanted to tell Dave about. I just about fell out of the rocking chair! It was time for me to get him some information. He said he was looking at another marketing company that was just going crazy, but he had not joined. I asked him if I could overnight a video to him and urged him to not join anything until he talked to Dave.

Later that night he signed up over the phone and booked a meeting in Nebraska for the following Tuesday. It was a four-and-a-half hour drive. Dave was so excited. He got on the phone and helped Shawn sponsor his dad. Shawn's dad was the person who had given Dave the book, *Psycho-Cybernetics,* that so changed his way of thinking and his life. We had a pair! We still needed a few more, but that was a lot more fun than motivating the ones who had been in the business since

February. I made calls for the rest of the night, and even talked to my dad in South Dakota. I mentioned to him that there were people making a tremendous amount of money in South Dakota, and he actually had met some of them on his truck-driving route. He said he would look at it, but it wasn't going to help me out with my deadline.

I was at the Elks Club that week at our local meeting and the room was filled with people from all over the state. There was a farmer and his wife from Holyrood, Kansas. They were there with a lady that I was surprised had even enrolled, but she was in. I had heard the phrase, "Little hinges open big doors," and they must, because the lady who brought this couple had a hard time covering a check for a haircut at my salon. Many times she would make payments on a $10.00 account. How did she find the money to join? How did she find this couple that was so excited? I had no idea, but I knew she was excited as they shared their experience being involved in Amway years ago and their belief in network marketing. They asked me about the meeting in Salina next week rather than the one set for tomorrow, and looked forward to seeing me there. Thank goodness, there would be one new person coming to that meeting that was seventy miles from home.

Our charts were on the wall, and we were dying to get those circles filled. It just wasn't coming together. We had a meeting the next night in Salina. I brought a guest from a rural town between Russell and Salina, and she signed up. She had mentioned the meeting to a friend who came on the spur of the moment, and she signed up! We were just a couple of people away from our goal.

I needed one person to join and to get one under them. Just before midnight I joined under Dave and sponsored the girl from the meeting as my personal instead of his. We hit our goal by midnight! We were Platinums! There were less than 300 Platinums in the entire company, and we were invited to go on a cruise to the Bahamas! We were exhausted, but the feeling of accomplishment was worth it. I couldn't believe that we did it, but then again, giving up was not an option for us. We had to make a decision during this time to either have a breakdown, or a breakthrough, and it was just a decision.

Lesson Learned:

> *"When you set a goal in writing and make a commitment with a deadline, it becomes so real that failure is not an option. You have no choice. It has to happen!*

13

I'm Going to Make Them Eat Those Words

I AM NOT SURE WHY it is usually the people we love the most who say the things that cut the deepest. Surely people don't mean to be cruel, but often they are. If it weren't for the books and the tapes, I am not sure where Dave and I might be today. We stayed focused, even on the days it was almost impossible to face the public and go to work, let alone drive to one more meeting.

The girl from the flower shop stopped by the shop to let us know that everywhere she went someone was handing out a flyer warning the locals that there was a SCAM coming through town. I was sure that they weren't talking about our company, but as I read it, it was definitely us they were targeting. Dave's Mom called to say that the same flyer was in every mailbox at the hospital, and people were starting to panic. There was nothing I could do.

I looked at the calendar as we started the new week so I could plan my sitters, meals, and days at the salon. It would be a short week but a busy one. Dave was heading west, and I was heading east. Starting tonight we had two weeks straight of home meetings or meetings at cafes, hotels, and community centers. I was hesitant to go back to Salina since I had been no-showed a couple of times. We traded, and I took Quinter, Kansas. We couldn't cancel Salina in case one person might be there, so Dave agreed to go and show the plan. As I was leaving town, I filled up my car with about $20 in gas. I went inside the local gas station to pay as a young kid pumped my fuel and cleaned my windows. There were only two pumps, but it was the busiest spot in our little town. It became deadly quiet as I walked in to pay, and I wondered why with all of the coffee drinkers in their booths that were usually filled with chatter. I handed the man my cash and leaned over the glass counter to get a pack of gum and noticed a newspaper clipping under the glass that held the candy. The newspaper clipping was front and center as if it were a warning that said NO CHECKS or something very important. It took me by surprise as I read the yellow highlighted section and saw my husband's name in bold print, announcing the financial mistakes we had made and the amount of money we owed to each person. I wanted a superhero to fly down and rescue me, or the people in the store to vanish so I could escape what seemed like a pack of wolves around me. I paid for my fuel, acting like I didn't notice. I got in my car to drive away and I cried. I felt like it was impossible for me to go face people at a meeting and tell them how they could become financially free. I believed in the business and I knew that many people were making money. I just had no idea how someone like me, who felt like such a failure, could lead anyone. I hated myself, and I was starting to hate other people.

I remembered a tape that was in one of our monthly trainings titled "I am Going to Make Them Eat Those Words," and the title meant more to me that night than at any other time I had listened to it. Rejection is hard to take when people tell you "no" and even harder when people justify why they don't believe in you or your company. It's not just the person telling you "no" that hurts. When someone doesn't say "yes" you start to wonder what is wrong with you. There is nothing wrong with you! It is that person's own decision whether your opportunity is something they want to pursue. I didn't realize it at the time, but it was a good thing those naysayers weren't in my business. They would have sucked the life out of all of the good people who made a decision to join our team. Everything happens for good. I do believe that, but I wish I had known then that my success was guaranteed. What if this didn't work like I thought and I had egg on my face in front of my home town? How would I ever live there and raise my children?

It was dark out. It seems like when the sun goes down, our fears are a lot worse than they are when it is day time. I was alone driving in my car, and I wanted to turn around and go home to my kids and sit in a chair and cry. I knew I couldn't cancel the meeting. I had to be a person of my word. I drove down I-70 to meet a room full of people I had never seen. It was a one-tape drive. I am not sure how I got there, because I don't remember any exits or any landmarks since I was deep in thought. I was furious and I agreed with the guy on the tape. The people in my home town, who were trying to tear me down, would eat their words. I would be successful in this even if it killed me!

There were about twenty-five people at the meeting at the Quinter Q Inn, and they all brought food for a potluck before the slide-show. I hated the slide-show. I thought my presentation was much more exciting, but the system said to show the slides, so I did. I had to add my stories between each slide to let the crowd know why each slide made so much sense. They didn't know me very well yet, but they were assured that I was there to support them. I talked about them and their dreams and convinced every person in the room that, together with our help, they would achieve anything they dreamed. I talked about our moms and how they were already seeing results. I told the story of the first girl who joined and did nothing and how we had spilled people under her. I talked about the things we would do together in the future and how everyone in that town would soon either be involved, or wish they were. With that, I ended the meeting and over a dozen people passed in their applications. I could not believe my eyes, and I could not believe that anyone could be inspired by someone going through so much emotional upheaval at home. But I believed in this business and they could see it!

I drove back home wishing I could reach Dave, but he did not answer. I couldn't wait to tell him what I had done. I decided not to share my experience at the gas station before the meeting with Dave; and even if I had to fill the truck with gas every day, I would not give Dave any reason to visit that gas station. I had to find a way to protect him from the pain and humiliation I had experienced. I checked the messages when I got home to see if there were any new people who had called, and to my surprise our car dealer, who was very successful, had called to let us know he was quitting. He mentioned that he had been warned about the scam and must return his stuff immediately. I had no idea what he was talking about. I was hoping I could change his mind. I quickly called and encouraged him not to let others stop him from succeeding, but it was too late. He and his wife had sent their box back immediately. I was sad, because when we were at their home showing them this business, they were both so excited. It hurt me to see people lose their dreams, but if they didn't believe it was going to work, it wasn't going to. You had to believe in what you were doing in order to get others to follow you.

Dave got home late but he had four people at his meeting. It was so tough to get that town going, yet there were ten times more potential people in Salina than in all of our rural groups that were erupting with new executives. Dave had set another meeting and promised them I would be there. I had to go back with hopes that four would turn into at least five or six. This was our third trip there without much growth. It was tough to justify the sitter, the gas, and the meals, but we were persistent.

The FedEx man greeted us at the door the next morning as we turned on the Espresso sign and lit a few candles to freshen up the store. Dave and I were fighting over the envelope. It had to be a huge check! We had worked so hard. It was two thousand and four dollars payable to David Pitcock! I wished my name was somewhere on the check. After all, I was his partner by now! I hugged him, and we started calling our friends to see if they had their checks yet. This was not nearly as much as we needed, but it was growing, and so were we. Most of the people were excited to see that our checks were going up. Of course, there were those who hadn't done anything yet who wondered why they hadn't received a check in the mail. That bothered me. I couldn't have anyone unhappy in my group. My biggest goal was to make sure everyone started making money, and I was sure I was good enough to get four for everyone, even if they didn't put in any effort. I started to call people for other people, and in some cases I gave people away. I made a decision to spend half-days at home on the phone and half-days at the salon. There was better money in a one-hour presentation that brought a "yes" than an eight-hour day at the salon. We were building up to the big meeting in Hays with our upline and top money earner of the company.

Weekly meetings in our little home town started to grow to fifty and sixty people. Sometimes people would invite someone that didn't come, and the next week they would show up with another person. It was like a competition to see who could get to people first. Unfortunately there were people who had animosity towards others, and in one particular case, it was my sister who got the raw end of the deal. I couldn't play favorites and do something for my family that I wouldn't do for others. I encouraged the couple to sign up under the person they felt they could work with the best. It was hard to know what to do when there were so many people showing up and many of them had the same friends. Everyone was signing up! I was trying to make everyone happy, and I realized I couldn't. Sometimes there were so many people joining, others would argue over who should be the sponsor. From then on I encouraged them to follow the rule to sign up under whoever invited you first. Groups were growing so fast! People would come to the meetings. They would see the checks of others or hear their success stories, and fear of loss had them signing at the back of the room immediately. We were almost scared because success was coming. We knew it meant even more responsibility.

We needed more meeting givers. Dave and I were running ragged, and we wished we knew how to get others to do what we were doing. I couldn't wait for someone else to buy tools and give them away or rent meeting rooms so I didn't have to. I was sure there were people qualified to do it, but for some reason they all wanted Dave or Barb.

I was at the Elks Club again that week at our local meeting and the room was filled with people from all over the state. I showed the plan to the room full of people and told the stories as I had told week after week, in the same dress I had worn night after night. The dress was brown with an Indian print and it had beads hanging from the neckline; I hand washed it every morning so it would be dry by night for my next meeting. It was a sundress that I had bought on a clearance rack, and to me it was dressy. As I told the story, I kicked my right leg and bent my knees simultaneously splitting the rotten cotton dress from my knee clean up to my hip. I had literally worn it to shreds! We took an immediate break for testimonies while I ran to the restroom in shear embarrassment, begging anyone for a safety pin or two. I finished the meeting as quickly as I could and told them that when you are excited, the facts don't count, "Just get in!"

Some joined, some laughed, and some said they would try to come up with the money. Each meeting had a difficult person asking questions like, "Is this a pyramid?" I was becoming pretty good at managing difficult people, and I could turn a conversation around in a New York Minute to find the positive and persuade them to see how it just made sense to join. I had no idea what I was doing, but I believed in this business with all of my heart. I was on fire, and so were most of the people who got around me.

Our weekly Salina meeting often was a no-show or was very small but we were dedicated and continued to go for anyone who might be there. We went back the following week and that night we had over fifty people in the room! Craig and Debbie Mog, the farm couple from Holyrood, Kansas, who had been at the Russell meeting sponsored eight people that week and they brought them all to the meeting! It was like popcorn in hot grease! Our business was going crazy! People were getting in by leaps and bounds.

I couldn't wait to get another paycheck. I just knew it would be ten thousand dollars by next month, and I needed it now. I was more obsessed than ever and began to work harder. I called more people and booked more meetings than I had ever before. Dave was worse than me. He was rarely in his shop anymore. He was either on the phone with a new person or our sponsor. We talked with our sponsor daily, and if we weren't feeling up-beat when the phone rang, we were up by the time we hung up. Our upline was calling us with questions like, "How in the heck are you guys doing it?" "It's called work," Dave would say. We are working this every single day as if it were a business, and it was going to grow to be bigger than any business we had ever built. Many of the people in our upline were just doing this part time here and there, but their checks were exploding because of our efforts. Some of them were making eighteen to twenty percent commission from our group's sales and Dave and I were barely making ten percent at this point. We were out of videos, and our upline from South Dakota shipped us one hundred videos overnight. He told us to put the check in the mail. The total was $750.00 for the tools, and we planned to go through them as fast as we could. It was the tool flow through our group that was creating the growth. It wasn't easy to invest that kind of money. In fact, some people thought that was expensive. My reply to them was this: "You ought to try to build it without the tools. Now that is expensive!"

With the video in hand, people would leave a meeting and go show the plan to their friends. People who were six states away were joining our group and then looking for a meeting in their area. Many times there were no meetings close to them, so we would hold conference calls.

Our house was like Grand Central Station and people were coming to the door early morning to all hours of the night. My kids were usually in diapers or running around stark naked! I couldn't keep clothes on them. They thought it was funny to show off as the people came to the door, and I was usually wondering if our downline thought I was an unfit mother. My house was still torn up like a tornado had just hit it, and it was in bad need of a makeover. Even a throw rug would have been a big improvement to cover up the underlay covered with the dried glue from the carpet we had torn up. I was anxious to get a big check and hire someone to come and help, because Dave had no time to finish the project he had started. For him to stop what we were doing might have cost us thousands of dollars. Other people wouldn't even have a meeting until they got their garage cleaned up or their yard mowed. We showed the plan all day. Our place was starting to look like it was condemned, but we didn't care. We were showing the plan, showing the plan, and showing the plan! Our upline talked about being obsessed with the business, and I was starting to understand that term.

You have to learn to be flexible if you want to be rich! Eating at a certain time, going to bed at a certain time, mowing on a certain day, or keeping your normal routine, may not be possible when you are building momentum. Just focus on the activity that will make you grow. If it is not an income-producing activity, don't do it until your business is at a point you feel comfortable. My motto was this, "A clean house is the sign of a stagnant distributor." That made it easier for me to justify that I was far from organized. I knew my house was never unbearable, but it not what I was used to before this network-marketing business.

The big day was coming! Our upline would soon be in town to show the plan. It had been three months since we joined the business and we had focused on it for ninety days straight. There were about two hundred people in our group, but many of them were in levels so deep we did not get paid on those levels. We were lucky to have one hundred in our commission group. We needed to get to the next level to get paid at the Infinity bonus level. There was no cut-off on the commissions you could make, no matter how deep your organization grew, once you qualified for the Infinity bonus. This was part of the benefit to qualifying as a Platinum by convention and we were just six applications away! We had sponsored more than ten people by now, but only about half of them would allow us to help them build their business. Many of the people were just waiting to see what would happen. It was hard to convince them that success would not just attack them. They might have to do something. I was getting resentful that they wouldn't at least get one person sponsored. After all, we needed their help to get to the next level!

Help always came from a training tape just when I needed it—those words of encouragement that would straighten my little mind right out. "You can't push a rope, said my mentor. It's easier to give birth to new people than it is to raise the dead! Get up and quit trying to motivate your group, because if you stop personally sponsoring, so will they." And finally, one last question, "How many people does it take to become a Platinum?" His question had me confused, because I was doing the math and thinking about how many people we had to have and how many of them had to have one person enrolled. As I sat adding up the circles on the form and calculating the amount of people it would take, and how many I needed. "The answer is one!" he exclaimed. "It only takes you!" The tape would go from having me excited to having me in tears, and sometimes he made me so mad. He had a way of saying things that would make me feel so guilty I just wanted to let him know that if he was in my shoes, he could see it the way it really is. It was hard for my thick red head to admit when I was wrong, but I was wrong to blame others for my lack of success in reaching my pin level. Many of the people in our organization just wanted to buy products, or perhaps they got a spot just to try to build the business slowly. I wanted everyone to meet me at my level, which was 100 percent focus. I was fortunate enough to have a mentor and an upline in that company that didn't tell me what I wanted to hear, but rather what I needed to hear. Although he made me mad on many occasions, it always made me get into motion, made me take action.

I would get so excited after listening to training tapes that my attitude would always change. The sad thing about it is the ones who need to hear the tapes most were usually not the ones listening. They were the ones who would call me complaining. At first I took this personally, but later realized it was because they had not plugged into the system, thus they lost their fire, their focus, and their dreams. It's part of this business, and there is no way to avoid it. You need to be equipped with the tools to succeed. There will be some people who are hurt, and there will be some who are lost, and there will be some failures that you are not expecting. People quit. That's part of life, but it is their choice. Learning that there will be a percentage that do quit, and a percentage that won't, helped me. I realized that it was not me, that it was their loss. I did all I could do. They had the best support and a system to follow.

Our check came for the month of April, and it was the last part of May. It seemed to take forever to get those checks. We were always about five to six weeks out from each pay period. I just knew it would be ten thousand. It had to be! I had seen the growth charts of our friends in South Dakota, and many of them were making well over $10,000 at the level we had reached. We opened the check on the station in the salon, and to our surprise, it wasn't nearly the amount that we thought it would be. Our check was $4,000 for the month, and we had hoped it would be so much more. We needed it! When you need it, you tend to be desperate and that comes across when you speak to others. Our intention had to be that we were in this to help others. We knew that. Our own financial situation was at the point where if our check wasn't $10,000 a month we might not be able to survive much longer. We had made purchases of inventory, tools, advertising, and trailers. Of course, knowing that we would soon be rich, I bought a car that would get me to meetings. Not just any car, I had to get a Mark VIII Lincoln so I could impress the people with my vehicle. The decisions we made and the judgment we used had created our situation. Dave and I needed to do something quickly, and we knew it.

I went to lunch and when I came back, the white furniture trailer was parked in front of the store. Dave asked me if I cared if he wrote, "GOING OUT OF BUSINESS" across the front of it. I was scared but I agreed with him. It would take four hundred haircuts to make four thousand dollars. I figured full-time network marketing would be better than part-time, and we would soon hit our financial goals without having to go to work every day and without the overhead and the stress of the shops. We sold out within two weeks! We never went back to the shop.

Most people would have been ecstatic with $4,000 a month, but not us. Dave and I were disappointed. We had compared ourselves to others, and we set our goals so high that as we grew, it was never good enough. We beat ourselves up to the point that we were almost depressed.

The convention was coming. We paid for our other ticket out of our commission check. We used the rest to pay our bills and put some back for tools and tapes to build even bigger the next month. Dave bought some leads, which at that time were $60.00 a name. He was scared to death, but the leads were supposed to be very good. If he closed two out of ten at a thousand dollars, he could pay for the leads. Two out of ten was not very realistic for a beginner, but he did sponsor one or two people from other states and that built his confidence to call even more. We began to work local leads throughout the day, and if I was on the phone setting up meetings Dave would drive to meet the lead and show the plan.

Stacy, the girl who lived in the in the basement, was helping out a lot. After she came home from school she'd watch the kids for me for a couple of hours while I made calls. She worked at the local discount store at night, and when I didn't have a meeting, she liked to go out with her friends. Even when she watched the kids a little bit, it helped. Brooklyn looked like a little Precious Moments doll, and the babysitter adored her. She took Brooklyn and Chance for ice cream treats or to play at the city park. Brooklyn was growing quite independent. She loved her little brother, and he was almost as big as she was. She would push him in the stroller as if she was the caregiver of her little brother. "Bubby" was easier to say than Chance, and so he was "Bubba" to all who knew him. They colored on the walls while I was on the phone, and occasionally they thought it was more fun for them to go on the floor than in their diaper. I would pat them on the rear and tell them "No," but they would laugh like I was crazy or something. Usually I was on the phone, so I didn't discipline them like they needed, but there was never anything they messed up that I couldn't undo. I guess it would have been different if I had new walls and carpet, but it was almost as if we were living in a construction site.

Soon it was the night before the big night, our big meeting in Hays! It was late and Brooklyn and Chance would not go to sleep. They were wound up like a clock. I put their pajamas on and hoped to get them to sleep before Dave got home so we could have some of our sanity back.

Stacy mentioned to me that there was a negative article in the Russell newspaper pertaining to Dave and an outstanding bill. I didn't read the newspaper. Evidently she had been in a group people who had read it, and they wanted to warn her that we were up to no good. I stopped off at a newspaper machine to buy a local paper as Stacy and I drove those little toddlers around singing nursery rhymes and trying to lull them to sleep. I read the article. Sure enough, the dream stealers were after us again, but this time, they would not win!

I couldn't let Dave see this article. If he read it, he might not be able to stand in front of the crowd the next night and introduce the speaker. Dave was terrified of crowds, and he was already as nervous as he could be. We told each other everything. I could not keep a secret from him, but I could make sure he did not read a newspaper before tomorrow night! Stacy and I drove around town and bought every paper out of every vendor. She actually went and took the newspaper off of the sidewalk of anyone who might rain on Dave's parade. With our car full of Russell Daily News we headed to the City

Lake to have a bonfire all of our own. Stacy was well aware of how hard we were working, and yet she heard the opinions of so many people being cynical of our pursuit of happiness. We took great satisfaction in burning every newspaper we could buy or find and professing that nothing was going to get us down. We were determined to succeed.

Once again, I was determined as I hugged Stacy and refused to give in to the naysayers and their opinions. We watched the papers burn as we cried and exclaimed that phrase of determination, "I'm going to make them eat those words!"

14

A Single Event Can Change Your Life: the Phrases You Hear, or the People You Meet

THE KANSAS WIND WAS BLOWING, and it was a hot summer day as we drove to Hays with anticipation of a big meeting. Although we were supposed to introduce the speaker, it was hard for us to get away early. Our car was packed with people excited about hearing the speaker. Dave and I had extolled the guy coming to town as if he was right next to God, because he had made such a difference in our lives. As we invited our friends to come and listen, we knew he could make a difference for them, too.

Dave did a great job introducing the speaker and welcoming the crowd. He was so nervous, but I don't think anyone could tell. There were over four hundred people in the seats and some overflowing into the hallway. We were just hoping they would all get in the room! Some were in the back of the room excited as ever, and others were there just to let you know why it wouldn't work and what their theory was. We made a decision to get them out of the halls and into the seats, and to get the meeting started right on time. I was shaking in my shoes. I had just dragged over a dozen people to hear this guy, and he better be good! My grandma was pushing seventy-years-old, but she was in the seats, along with her daughter who didn't have the money to join but thought it was exciting. Dave's grandma, along with his mom, his dad, and every other relative we could get there were also in attendance. My sister and her husband were one of my biggest naysayers in the beginning. They had come to our house one night for a haircut and I had put in the video. Not only did my sister sign up, but her husband got his own spot, too. This was their first meeting.

It was hard to get close to the speaker. Prior to the meeting his limo had dropped him off at the hotel. He had a body guard next to him who was carrying a walkie-talkie with an earplug attached; he was more than intimidating. I hoped I would at least get to meet our mentor before he left.

I could not believe how many people were at the meeting, but looking back over the last three months, we had been promoting this as we showed the plan almost every single night of the week and on weekends, too. It would all pay off very soon!

As they listened to the stories he told, the entire crowd was in stitches. I thought he would be all polished with his Armani suit and alligator shoes, but he really connected with the people right off the bat.

There wasn't much of a limo service in Hays, Kansas. He joked as he told the story of how the limo died in the airport parking lot. The driver told him to hang tight while he got out to check under the hood. The wind caught the hood and sprang it to the point that he worried it might come off. They had to call a service truck to jump the battery. They pulled off after they jumped the battery, but within a few blocks the limo died again. It took a while for them to get there, but they finally made it. We knew these were just normal small-town things you put up with when you don't live in Chicago or Kansas City.

Although we were small town, we had dreams bigger than people in most cities he had visited, and he made that very clear. People were nodding their heads and laughing long before he talked about the company. He spoke highly of our upline, and praised Dave and me for all of our hard work. He did more than show the program. He let everyone in the room know that they could do it. Then after a short thumbnail sketch, he created an urgency and most people there were scared not to join.

The meeting was over and people had applications ready to sign up their prospects. One of our groups from way out west hit a new pin level that night. We knew that leaders were born because we had promoted that function. The amazing thing was that no matter how good the speaker was some of the people just didn't get it. In fact, many were worried they couldn't afford to use the products they were required to purchase each month. To us the only question was, "If we had the potential to make $500.00 a month, would we switch where we shopped and spend $100.00 of our dollars each month with our own company?" It was common sense to use the products and be able to take advantage of the tax breaks we had from owning our own home-based business. Yet some were worried they might make too much and not be qualified for their welfare benefits. It proved to me, no matter how good the speaker is, not everyone will get it! The presenter can't say the wrong thing to the right person. On the other hand, the presenter can't say the right thing if he is speaking to the wrong person. It was hard to leave some of our friends behind, but I figured if this man couldn't convince them, nobody could.

It's never how many people you have in your company. It's how many you can get to attend the events. Whether the event is a home meeting, training, or a major convention, that is where the future of your business lies.

The meeting was over. Many of the people hung around, but the speaker had disappeared. Dave and I tried to find where he had gone, and then we noticed his assistant was in the hallway near a hotel room by the pool. He was changing for the flight home. The private jet was waiting at the airport and his driver would be there soon.

We went back to the ballroom to gather our belongings and applications and assumed we would not get to visit with him. Just as the last people were leaving, he came there to visit with us before he left. We were numb. I had never had anyone in my upline like him take time to listen or talk to me. He talked with us about our business and said he noticed we hadn't sponsored anyone new the previous month. We admitted that we were a little hung up about the fact that we had worked so hard and our checks were not where we wanted them to be. He looked us straight in the eye and said, "When was the last time you personally started a new group? That is the Rx for everything: starting a new group and sponsoring someone new." He spoke about where the company was headed and about his vision. He encouraged us to get to the convention, and said he would see us there. He told us we could do it. With that, he left, and we were more committed than ever.

We didn't sleep a wink that night. We only wished we had done more, had more personals there, and had him coming back again. There was another group that had driven there from Nebraska that night, and we did not want them moving in on our territory. We wanted to own the midwest in this company, and we wouldn't settle for anything less. That was the summer of 1996. In our first ninety days in the business we had laid a solid and amazing base and we would never regret having worked so hard to achieve it.

Wheat harvest season was a busy time in Kansas and many people were busy in their fields. Our house was a mile from the grain elevator where farmers dumped their wheat for storage. The pilot from that meeting held in the single-wide trailer showed up at our door. I hadn't seen him for a while, but he had eight applications in his hand and said he had more coming. He had been showing the plan in the dust on the hood of the farm trucks ... drawing circles while he waited in line at the grain elevator. His punch line was, "You can't even replace a tractor tire for the amount it takes you to get started ... look at the money we put into farming in order to make a profit!" He had introduced Dave to one couple from Quinter back in March, and because we had focused on helping them, his checks were over $750.00 a month.

There was power in the plan if you worked it, because everyone would benefit from the monthly residual income. We did a lot in the beginning that it didn't seem like we were getting paid for, but now, as new leaders in this company, we were getting ready to get rewarded in ways that we had not yet even imagined. There was no limit to what a person could do as they helped others become successful.

The summer went by and our checks didn't grow like we thought they would, but they were steady. We had focused a lot of our time on helping other people, and many of them were not people we were getting paid for since some were 18 levels deep in our organization. There were more people out of our pay lines than in our seven-level pay lines, but we helped everyone, knowing that it in time our efforts would be rewarded.

In the compensation plan we had at that time, until you achieved the rank of Diamond you were paid for people only seven levels deep in your 4 x 7 matrix. It was tough to drive the miles for distributors who were eighteen levels deep in our organization knowing we would not be compensated for our time and travel expenses. We believed we had to go and help all of those outside of our seventh level, because we knew it would build stability for our group and our future income. Even though we sometimes felt resentful when we were making sacrifices, including leaving our children while building outside of our seventh level, we knew that once we were Diamonds the Infinity bonus would be well worth all of our current time and effort. The Diamond Infinity Bonus paid a percentage of all product movement outside of our seventh level—and on to infinity. We knew that would be huge! So, we never said "no" to a meeting unless we had somewhere else to be. We cared about everyone in our organization and were totally committed to their success!

Convention was coming! I had to get a new dress—one that would not split out from too many washings and that wasn't for maternity. I was so glad to be able to plan a trip with my husband, and our moms were willing to watch the kids. At this point in time, we weren't sure how we would get there. Cindy had a gas card we could pay off next month, and mom offered us her car, because it did better on gas than a dually diesel 4x4 truck.

We headed out in my mom's Lincoln and our friends were flying to Chicago to meet us at the convention, all two of them. We had to share a room with them, which wasn't too romantic, but it would be good for building relationships. As we drove to Chicago, I felt a little sick. I figured it was just my nerves. I couldn't imagine what it would be like.

When we got there the parking lot of the hotel was filled with dream cars. There was a Provost Motor Coach with a Vette on a trailer behind it. The Rolls Royce in the parking lot had a tag that read TMG, which stood for the initials of their business. I couldn't help but notice that most of the people walking in were very happy, very energetic, and some of them looked like they were movie stars. I begged Dave to take a picture in the parking lot, but he said we would look like Kansas hicks on vacation. Needless to say, we didn't stop. I wanted a photo by this Q45 Infinity. It was awesome with gold trim all over it. I loved it. It didn't make much sense to get a photo by your dream car when you drove your mother's car to convention. We had to get checked in and hoped our check would be sufficient. We didn't have one credit card left.

As we checked into the Hyatt in Chicago, I heard many voices that sounded familiar from training tapes, but I didn't dare stare or ask them for an autograph.

Our friends were going to be landing at Chicago O'Hare so we had to get checked in quickly. The event would begin at 4:00PM for us because we were Platinums. Everyone else would meet at 7:30PM tonight. We checked into our hotel, and I felt like Julia Roberts in *Pretty Woman.* Except for the tub, the rest of the room looked a lot like the one in that movie. I was used to motels where you entered from the outside, not through a long hallway with elevators on the inside and plush carpeting leading you down the hall to your room. There was even a basket of free apples at the desk. I took two, knowing full well Dave didn't like fruit. I was like a kid in a toy store, and it felt so good to be away.

We drove through major traffic, and I worried that Dave might go crazy by the time we got to the airport. We found American Airlines on a sign, and we quickly pulled into a spot right at the curb. I couldn't believe there was a spot available, but right ahead it said, "NO PARKING/TOW ZONE." I thought it would be fine since we would only be there a minute. Our friends were probably waiting on us. We locked the doors and ran in to find them. Looking down the hall we could see the luggage coming onto the belt from their flight. They came running to hug us and thank us for the ride. Just as we turned around to show them the way to the car, the tow truck passed the plate-glass window, towing a black car with Kansas tags. It was us! We had been towed away, and the car was headed for impound. It wasn't like we had ever been to the city before. We didn't realize how serious they were about towing your car away if you park in the wrong area, but it was too late now.

We took a taxi and all of their luggage to the impound where the guy had to laugh at my story. I told him how we were so naive to believe it would be fine to park in that zone and that our friends were meeting us for a convention. To make a long story short, I wrote him a check for $250.00 to get the car out of impound, and I made $300.00 from the signed applications from him and his friend. They were more excited about joining me in my new business than they were working for the impound agency at the airport, and they were looking forward to getting their starter kit. It was a good day after all! Everything happened for a reason. I wasn't going to let the airport security ruin my day!

We ran back to the hotel, trying to get there in time for our Leadership Briefing. Dave and I both had been anticipating the honor of being in the presence of the top three hundred people in the company. I could tell Dave was nervous. He didn't say much, but he was making sure we were in the last row and almost the last to enter the meeting room. There they were right up front, all of the RICH people! The people from the video were in some of the same suits I had seen them wear in the video, and my favorite lady from South Dakota had on a smashing white suit. I hadn't met her yet, but I knew her first name was Jody. Her tape had taught me about the money tree in the backyard. She had turned my entire business around and didn't even know it. I owed her so much. I had to tell her "thank you"!

The couple we had ordered the videos from sat right in front of us. We hadn't met them yet either, but Dave reminded me we owed them close to a thousand dollars. He was anxious to meet them but didn't want to have them ask us about the videos. Dave wrote out a check as we sat there, waiting to hand it to them after the meeting. How would we afford that? I didn't want to ask him. I knew he would be mad, but I was wishing I was the one in control of that checkbook. He was constantly reinvesting in our business, which was something I was always afraid to do.

Our upline was a man who had done infomercials on television. He was the independent distributor who was blamed for being a con-artist, and an ex-con, and credit card fraud was his crime. We had that going for us! The crazy thing was that everyone in the room was talking about the story tape of him and a young kid who was in jail with him, and how they turned their lives around and became millionaires in this company. Wow, thinking about my dad's side of the family, if people in prison could get out and become millionaires, there might be a chance for all my aunts and uncles! The feeling that I got was that it doesn't matter what you have been through in your past, it is your future that matters.

As this man asked everyone to take a seat, Dave was in awe. This was the guy we had met in Hays. This was the guy on all of our tapes, and he met with us for two hours before to the convention. What he said was like gold to Dave. I was hoping he wouldn't tell Dave anything I disagreed with. I thought I was such an expert from my past experiences. Sometimes I was a little hard headed when it came to building this business. This man was focused on taking this company to a hundred million in sales by the end of the year. He laughed about the press, the news, the *Wall Street Journal* articles, and all of the adversity that the company had experienced throughout the past few months. He said that not everyone is a big enough leader to handle the scrutiny and the road bumps along the way, but those of us in the room, we were the cream of the crop. I felt like jumping up and screaming a big Baptist, "Amen!" I didn't do anything, but I nudged Dave about everything he said. "You have to be willing to do things others will not be willing to do in order to have things that others will never have. Some days you are going to want to quit, and I will guarantee you a year from now, when we meet, there will be a lot of faces in this room that can't handle it, and they won't be in the next convention meeting." Dave looked over and on a paper he wrote, "We will be, and we will be 4-stars!" Everyone was screaming and clapping, saying, "I'll be here!" and he laughed with a comment of, "The ones who scream the loudest are sometimes the first to quit!" The purpose of the meeting was to speak to the leaders who were trying to lead a group. A lot of things he said made so much sense. It was like he had been in our house.

Dave took a notebook full of notes, and I realized why it was a "Leadership" meeting. There was no fluffing it. This was for the people who were serious about their business. Commitments like "never miss a function, always order three hundred in products, never quit adding to your list, invest ten percent of your income into personal development, give away ten percent of your income, always keep your trunk full of recruiting tools and products you can give away, and before you leave, make sure you sign up to go to California in the spring." Whoa! I wasn't rich yet, and obviously these people were.

He told a story told about a car salesman, and I remember it like it was yesterday.

There was a car salesman who struggled every month to make a sale. Every other car salesman had people returning to him to buy another car along with referrals of all of their friends. He ran ads, had business cards, and would even race to meet each new person on the lot, but he couldn't sell a car to save his soul. This particular car salesman was pretty discouraged, and in the sales meeting he sat at the back of the room trying to figure out what it was he was doing wrong.

At the end of the meeting the dealership owner, who was very successful, was advising them to attend a conference coming up in a few months for the most successful car dealers. The Car Salesman Conference was in California. "California?" thought the car salesman. "I can't go all of the way to California! Do you know how much that would cost? Do you know how far that is? Do you realize what it would take to get to California?" It was absurd for them to think that a car salesman with no success could sign up to go to California.

The dealership owner finished his meeting, and at the end he said, "Some of you are probably thinking you'll be more committed when you have more money, when you sell more cars, or after you've learned how to increase your commissions. The challenge is I know that those of you with the smallest checks will be the first ones to say, "It's too far, it's too expensive, and he is crazy for thinking I could go to California!" He ended his speech with, "That's why you will always be broke!"

At the end of the story about the car salesman, Dave and I nudged one another and made a commitment to get to California! There was no question. We did not want to stay broke.

There was food, drinks, and lots of extra perks for those of us attending that meeting. We got our own folder for the weekend that had the company logo on it, and I was so excited to go to our room and tell our friends what they missed at that Platinum Leadership Club!

As the meeting adjourned, we stood in the room waiting to get photos with all of the people who had many leaders in their groups and were making thirty thousand dollars, forty thousand dollars, and even one hundred sixty thousand dollars per month. I got their autographs all over my folder, and we asked them to take pictures with us to take back to our group. The main event was tonight, and the speaker was some guy I had never heard of. I was hoping that the Leadership Meeting would never end.

The Rosemont Theatre was the convention's home, and it was like going to a Broadway show or a large opera theatre. It was such a beautiful place! The red carpet was rolled out for the top leaders, and the seats were all full. Dave and I sat in the far back row of the main level. The balcony was packed, and we were at the top of the second level of the theatre. To the right was a door for only those of us who had made it to the leadership level. They served a few drinks in that room and, of course, there were company products available for our use.

The music was so loud we could hardly hear each other talk. We had a death-grip on each other's hands as we walked down the aisle to our seats. The master of ceremonies for the event was like a professional speaker. I couldn't imagine how nervous he must be. I was just glad we didn't have to appear for the ceremony until the next night, because just to say our names would send me into tears. I was so emotional that all I wanted to do was cry. It was like I was in a dream I didn't ever want to wake from.

The speaker was a man by the name of Les Brown and that was a name I had never heard. He was a black man, and when he took the stage all he could do was laugh ... and everyone in the crowd laughed right along with him. It was contagious, and it felt so good. He told his story that night, and I cried for the entire hour of his keynote speech.

To this day, it is my favorite convention speech and the title has grown very famous, "It's Not Over, Until I Win." I took pages of notes, but many of my notes were on a paper with tear stains that made it hard to read. It was like he was talking to me. I had no idea a convention for a nutritional company would change my life in so many ways. Les spoke of his disappointments, his fears, his setbacks and, of course, his victories. He had a way of making me feel like I deserved to win. He was so moving that people were standing on their feet clapping as he finished with, "It's not over, no, no—it's not over, until I win."

Dave and I were in awe of him, holding onto each other's arms as tightly as we could. If that wasn't enough, the president of the company followed him. I listened to every word, and for the first time since we had joined the business, I realized this was about more than just making money … we were changing people's lives.

We didn't sleep at all that night. We sat up and talked to the couple that met us there until the sun was coming up, and then we took turns using the shower and headed down for the morning session.

I didn't really know much about the products, but there were sure a lot of product people there. I was learning a lot just networking in the bathroom during the breaks. People had products in their purses and some had them in little samples. We had hardly used the products, and yet we were making thousands of dollars per month. I thought to myself, "Just imagine if we knew how good the products were!" Maybe we should learn more about them. We sat through the product sessions and I must say we were pretty impressed. Since we were 23 and 24 years old, we didn't have many health issues, but we found a few products we believed we could get excited about. There were products for kids, and a weight-loss product that I was pretty excited about. After being pregnant for two years, I was ready to get my waistline back.

One of the eight steps we were taught in order to achieve financial freedom was to "Use the Products." I used the products, and we loved the energy products and the personal care items. I had even put the shampoo in my salon. Knowing I could have made more buying the wholesale stuff at the beauty supply store, I decided instead to make my brand the one from this company. I didn't really know how this step could affect my income level but I would follow the steps.

A man by the name of Charlie Tremendous Jones took the stage after the break. He was so funny. He talked really fast, and he laughed in between each sentence. It was healthy to laugh after all of the emotion from the evening before. His book was *Life Is Tremendous* and he was dancing around like a doll that was wound up too tightly for the key to unwind. He made a comment about his mentor, Ed Foreman, being in the seats at the convention. These people were a big deal, and they were in the same company as me. Maybe I wasn't crazy if they were in it as well. It was a good thing we were doing it. Dave just loved this speaker as he talked about the importance of books throughout his entire talk. I did not have time to sit around and read, and I was not making up excuses. I was busy. He said that *Leaders* are *Readers*. According to Charlie Jones, "You will become the total of the books you read, the people you meet, and the tapes you listen to." I loved the tapes and I was trying to meet the people, but they were a long way from my home town. Charlie joked about husbands and wives and relationships, along with people who are difficult to deal with. Everything he said made so much sense. We decided we would "Laugh about it now. You are going to laugh about it ten years from now!"

Charlie ended his speech with a standing ovation and people were rushing to the stage to get his autograph. This was my first time to hear of him, and obviously he was a world renowned speaker and author. We ran to the hallway to get in line to purchase his album before the people up front got to the table. Fortunately for us, his escort took him through the crowd to his table in the hallway, and we were first in line. We shook his hand and he signed his book for us. He told us we were a sharp couple and he was so lucky to get to meet us. I thought he was going to kiss Dave, but instead he just held his hand and talked straight into his eyes. He told me I was "perty," and that is just how he said it, "perty." He reminded me of my grandpa who used to sing about my freckles being "perty." What a character, changing people's lives!

The top money earners spoke during the afternoon about focus and definiteness of purpose. We were calling people during the breaks, and we must have sounded like babbling idiots. It was hard to call home and explain what we were experiencing. By the end of the session, Dave was convinced we needed a photo of that car. During the break as we went back to the hotel to change, we spotted the car. There I was practically on the hood, and Dave was hoping security wouldn't spot him next to the car. We were laughing hysterically, and like our mentor had taught us, we didn't say, "I want this car." We said, "This is mine, and I'm going to have it!" Try doing that a month or two after your car is repossessed! That felt pretty goofy, but they said it would work so we did it, no questions asked.

We quickly changed into our "formal" wear, which for Dave consisted of black jeans, a western jacket and a bolo tie. I wore a plain black dress that was just a sleeveless sundress and black heels. There was a beautiful CZ necklace in the gift shop located in the lobby of the hotel. I really wanted it and it was less than fifty bucks, but that would have put us short to get home. I didn't feel too "successful" living paycheck to paycheck, and it might have been easier if we hadn't quit our jobs so soon. They said it was a "part-time" business, but we figured if we went full time, we would get it done even quicker. I think it hurt us to quit our jobs, because we took ourselves out of the loop of people. Not only did we not see anyone all day, we had so much time on our hands, it was easy to analyze everything and get hung up about stuff that was really no big deal. Idle time is not a healthy thing, and busy people definitely get more done. I had a lot to do, but so much of it was non-income producing. I made commitments that weekend to live below my means, pay off debt, and not to buy "stuff" unless it would help me build my business. I felt a little queasy the next morning, but I thought it was probably just from the handshake and hug in front of 6,000 people clapping. We didn't even have to talk; our names were announced as we entered the stage with the other 300 Platinums. That was the greatest feeling in the world and I wished it would never end.

We had a long drive ahead of us, and that would give Dave and me the time to talk while our friends took a two-hour flight home. We had about sixteen hours to drive, and we hadn't had that much sleep since the night we left. We had a lot of tapes to listen to that we bought at the event, and that would make the time go fast.

I missed my babies. We had never left them for three days straight. I had no idea how we would go on the cruise in January, but I was committed to do whatever it took. They were my reason for working so hard, and soon I would make all of their dreams become a reality. I could see us at Disney World in Orlando with Chancey jumping up and down with Tigger, and Brooklyn dancing around with Cinderella. I missed them badly.

As we got in the car to drive home, I started to look over my pages of chicken scratches and bold underlines, along with asterisks and an occasional big exclamation mark. The notes from Les

Brown had my head so full it felt like a fire hose was in my mouth. These quotes were just a few I reflected on, and we talked about them all the way home.

"If you help others achieve their dreams,
you will achieve yours."

LES BROWN

"How it is going to happen is none of your business ...
while you are making excuses, you are saying: but you don't
have my problems, but I am not smart, but I am not talented,
but you don't know me .... But, but, but. What you need to
do is just get your but out of the way!"

LES BROWN

"The person you become five years from now will be the
equivalent of the books you read, the tapes you listen to,
and the people you meet."

CHARLIE TREMENDOUS JONES

"We will be 4-Star."

SIGNED BY DAVID PITCOCK
(4-STAR WAS THE TOP PIN LEVEL OF
THAT COMPANY AT THAT TIME).

That was our focus from this point on. We were going to help everyone achieve their dreams and trust that ours would come true as a result. I was committed to get my buts out of the way and make this happen!

15

From Kansas to the Beaches of the World

I HATED TO LEAVE THAT CITY because I felt different when I was away from my home town. There was something about getting away from the people who knew everything I had been through and thought they knew everything I planned to do. In Kansas it was rare if you passed a car that was actually "new." If it was the current year's model, it might be a new farm truck or perhaps a Lincoln. There weren't many new homes within a two-hour radius of our town; and since oil prices had fallen most people were pretty pessimistic about the future.

Chicago was full of people from all walks of life. Les Brown talked so much about humiliation and feeling like a failure that I could finally laugh at some of the stupid mistakes I had made and know that someday I might still be a star. If he could survive being abandoned on a warehouse floor by his birth mother, and still grow to be a person who changed so many lives in one event, there was hope for me. The story of his talk show being cancelled made me think of the people who said we were scam artists. I must admit that of all the stories that stirred me, the one he told of making a commitment that his momma wouldn't have to scrub the floors of all of the rich people and take their leftovers home, was the one I really connected with. I cried just thinking about it. Here was my beautiful mom, on her hands and knees after working eight hours at the factory, cleaning houses just to put food on the table for the four kids that were still at home. She never complained, but I wanted to give her more. I often wondered how so many bad things could happen to such a good person, but that was a mystery not to be solved by me. She was my hero, and her work ethic was something I admired and tried to follow.

We drove as fast as we could to get home. I felt like I was car sick or had a case of the flu, but honestly I had felt this way the entire weekend. I thought it was probably just emotions. After all I should be dehydrated at this point from the tears I had shed during the event.

We drove through Indiana, Illinois, Missouri, and finally back to Kansas. The trees were beautiful as fall was approaching and the hot summer days would soon come to an end. Dave's mom was planning to open a furniture store in order to quit her job at the hospital and get away from the stress, the politics, and the hourly wage. She hoped to be open in time for the holidays. We were going to supply her with the solid oak reproduction inventory, so that would help us out a little while we built our group. We got home late that evening, and the kids were so happy to see us. As we pulled into the driveway, it felt good to be home, but then again, I didn't want the feeling I had to go away. I couldn't wait to get the album from the weekend. I was missing it already.

Our mailbox was full, the answering machine was blinking, and there were sticky notes on our door. The big envelope stuck in the doorway must be our check because it was the end of the month. Dave opened the check, and he didn't say much. He just set it down on the cabinet. I hoped it was just because he was tired, but my curiosity got me. The check had gone down over half. I couldn't understand how our check could go down. We had worked so hard, and it seemed like so many people were joining. The problem was that the two hundred people that just joined were outside of our pay lines, and we spent our whole month driving those groups. I noticed that many of our local people had a minus by their name, and there was no doubt the negative publicity from the flyers had done some damage. With no job to go to tomorrow and no paycheck other than this one, we definitely had some goals to set. I should have listened to our upline when he told us, "Don't quit your job until your paycheck is twice your income, and it is solid for at least six months." It was in spite of the people in Russell that we quit those five businesses, and it would be in spite of them that I would build this one. I started to doubt myself, and wondered why we had gone to Chicago and spent the money we needed so badly to pay our bills. I prayed that things would work out, and after all, this paycheck was from the prior month, not for the work I was doing right now. I was focused on increasing my income, but I had to help others get their dreams in order for that to happen.

The check lay on the table like a letter of bad news, and you would think we would have been thankful for residual income that was coming in every month. Nobody was to blame but us. We needed to personally sponsor new people every month and not just help our group. Nineteen hundred and ninety-nine dollars was the amount of the check. Our house and car payment were more than that combined, not to mention the cost of food and utilities. I made a list of people to call, and we made a decision to sponsor people for weekly checks. I took my notebook to bed with me, and my little Bubba rubbed my ear as he drank his bottle. Dave was quiet with Brooklyn snuggled up next to his chest. I prayed for him, because I knew he was thinking about our finances. It's important to me that money not be important to me. Reading the notes on my paper, I filled my mind before falling asleep reading quotes from Les Brown.

Les Brown:

"It's important to me that money not be important to me."

"Life has no limitations except the ones you make."

"If you view all the things that happen to you, both good and bad, as opportunities, then you operate out of a higher level of consciousness."

"Review your goals every day in order to be focused on achieving them."

"It's none of your business how it's going to happen, just believe it is going to happen."

"Some of you are saying But, you don't understand my situation, But I am so busy I don't have any time, But I don't have any time, but you don't know my situation, Les ..." Les Brown replied, *"What you need to do is get your Buts out of the way."*

I was so tired. I hoped I would wake up the next morning, and I prayed that Chance would sleep through the night so I didn't have to get up and go downstairs to make another bottle. Laying there watching both babies fall asleep made me think, it was always scarier at night when I would worry. Yet I was so thankful for everything I had right there in my arms. I loved my family.

Waking up without a job was a good feeling, but sometimes it took us until noon to really get our days started the way we used to. I unpacked our bags and started to do laundry, knowing full well that wasn't my most important priority, but it had to be done. The house was a wreck, but it would take a full day to clean that big two-story house, and I definitely did not have time for that.. My mom came by for her morning cup of coffee, and by noon Dave's brother stopped by for lunch. He just worked a few blocks away. It was convenient for him to have lunch with us and he loved to clean up the leftovers. He didn't really like his job changing tires at the Coop, but we had closed the store. We didn't have much work for him, so he had found another avenue for income. He didn't think he could do what we were doing, and quite honestly, sometimes I think he got sick and tired of hearing me on the phone through every noon hour and even when he stopped by after work. I never stopped talking. I was constantly talking to someone about the business trying to get them in the business.

Scott was four years younger than Dave and he was looking for the right girl. He always seemed like he might want to settle down but couldn't let anyone else know that. He loved to have a good time, and most of our lunch hours were stories of what happened the night before or the weekend before. Dave loved Scott so much he would always crack up at all of his stories, and then after Scott left we would sit there and shake our heads in amazement that he and his friends had all survived. They were crazy, but they were young. It was to be expected. He was one of the only people who called me Barbara, and he was one of the only people I knew who could grow hair down his back and come in looking like some kind of a wild man, but still have little kids run to him and flock around him like sheep that wanted to play. Chance and Brooklyn would roll around with Scott for his entire lunch hour, and he would bring them fake tattoos to put on while I prayed they wouldn't grow up and want real ones. The candy he brought them from the station was always a highlight for them, and it provided them with sugar to get them good and hyper enough to not want an afternoon nap. Scott played the drums, and when he came for lunch Brooklyn would drag out the Little Tykes Toy Drum set he bought her for her first Christmas. Chance would settle for all of my pots and pans with the wooden spoons and metal spatulas for a cymbal. Anything that entertained them was a break for me, but it was a little hard to visit with someone on the phone and have a homemade musical ensemble in the background. Chance would do anything for attention; he would jump off of the couch and roll as he landed or throw his bottle across the linoleum floor. He loved the fact that everyone would laugh at him. They were full of life by the time the noon hour was over.

Cindy's furniture store was opening this week. Dave and Scott were going to be unloading trucks after the run Dave made to Missouri and Texas to pick up furniture. It was always tougher when Dave was gone for several days. The kids were a lot of work, but one of the older ladies in our downline would come over and rock them as long as I was on the phone with her husband calling leads. That was my focus for the next few days. I would be stuck at home, but I would be working the phones.

I was getting frustrated as the days went by. All of the commitments we had made at convention seemed to be getting put on the back burner while we let other distractions take our time, our focus, and our energy. Even when Dave got back from Texas, it took several days from morning until night to get the store set up in the mall, which was approximately twenty-six miles from Russell. I was at home with two screaming kids day after day after day, and I became more than stir-crazy. I was not enjoying the so called "stay-at-home mom" title. Nobody had ever mentioned that a little bit of balance might be healthy, had they? Not me, I was 100 percent focused and obsessed with building the business. I was so angry. I got in my car and drove to the mall with both kids crying, and I rehearsed my speech the entire way to the mall. I needed Dave to help me get this business going. We were not getting any closer to paying our bills, and we had to take action, now! I had never felt such emotion, and I wondered why all I wanted to do was cry. When I entered the store, Cindy mentioned to me that I was a bit emotional and maybe needed to get some advice from a professional. She asked if there was a possibility that I was pregnant; she said the only time she had seen me like this was when I was at the beginning of each pregnancy when my hormones got a little out of whack. Perhaps a doctor's visit wouldn't hurt. I wasn't going to let someone else diagnose me as crazy, but it scared me not to check.

I went to my doctor in Great Bend the very next day. She was my baby doctor that been with me through Brooklyn and Chance. As a woman, I felt comfortable with her no matter what we talked about. I mentioned to her that I was on the verge of what most thought was a nervous breakdown. She asked me how the store was and if we were busy, and that was all it took. I gave her the low-down on all of the events that had taken place since November when Chance was born. She sat there with her mouth open in amazement that we had quit our jobs, and even more important, that we had joined a network-marketing company. She could see it in my eyes that this was different.

She told me how tired she was of the politics in her home town. She had delivered over four hundred babies the year Brooklyn was born, and now she was banned from the hospital saying she caused a child to die during delivery. We shared stories of people and their mentality when others rise to success, and she assured me that as long as we believe in what we do, we will succeed. She was in a long legal lawsuit herself, and said just because you get sued doesn't mean you are bad. It means you are in business.

In addition to her inspirational talk, she checked my heart, my throat, my blood pressure. It all looked good. It was then that she ordered a urine test, and said I would soon be on my way. It took her several minutes to return to the room, and when she did, she just hugged me and smiled. "You are going to be a mommy again!" she exclaimed. It was exciting news! I loved babies, and I always dreamed of having five. When Dave and I had our second child in two years, he had politely asked me to take my list of dreams that said "five kids" off the fridge and let us have a little break. Obviously taking it off the fridge didn't protect me from the results. I was going to have another little baby! I didn't know how I could possibly afford this, let alone have the energy to take care of it. Thinking of another little miracle like the two I had made everything else go away. I drove straight to the mall that was about an hour and a half from my doctor. I cried part of the way, and the two babies were fast asleep in their carriers in the back seat.

I was dreaming of what Brooklyn and Chance could be for Halloween and how I could dress them to match. Pooh and Tigger would be cute. Chance loved Tigger, and I could make the costumes. I hoped that our October check would be more than last month's, but hoping wasn't going to make it happen. I had to get busy! The mall was very slow. There was hardly a car in the parking lot. I had to question the sanity of my husband and his mom hoping that the holidays would bring them some people. It's easy to start feeling sorry for myself when the only people I had to communicate with were two toddlers under the age of two. I searched for the right words to say as I woke Brooklyn up to walk in and carried my little Bubba on my shoulder. Dave was sweating like a pig, unloading solid oak furniture, putting tables together, waxing the chairs and making price tags for the big grand opening that was coming soon. He wanted to help his mom. We would benefit in the long run, but it wasn't immediate income. He picked up Brooklyn and gave her a quick hug then got right back to working. I said, "I think we need to talk." Of course, when I told them I cried, and Dave laughed. He then hugged me assuring me that it was a blessing, and it would be awesome. Cindy took a big breath, and with her hands over her mouth said, "Oh Barb ..." She knew what pressure I was under and this was quite a surprise. We were all excited, and at least there was an explanation for my craziness. Knowing that I was pregnant, I went into immediate action mode and started putting together furniture myself. Now that it all made sense, I wasn't so mad. I was just a basket full of hormones on a roller coaster looking for a chicken exit, but there wasn't one.

That night Dave took off early, and we went home to that big house that was filling up more and more quickly. Dave thought it was just hilarious to blare Garth Brooks' song "Two of a kind, working on a full house!" as he ran the tub for him and the kids. We were so happy, and we were so in love. We just needed to get our business to the next level, and it needed to happen fast!

The monthly meetings in various towns were on the calendar, and so far we seemed to be the only two meeting givers that would commit to drive the distance and present the plan. There were a lot of people who were doing home meetings. We couldn't complain, but we needed more presenters than just Dave and me. The end of the month was near. To my disappointment I hadn't done a whole lot, but I had a week left to really get things going. I sat outside on the front porch admiring my neighbor's perfect little lawn as she planted her fall bulbs and wiped the faces of her tidy little children. My kids were up and down the block on their trikes. Brooklyn stopped to get the mail from two doors down and ran to me with the Richards' mail thinking she had done a good deed. Chance decided to give her some rocks to put in their mailbox so they would be surprised. It was a zoo at our house. My St. Bernard made a visit across the street while we were out, and he conveniently ran across the wet paint on the wrap-around porch that adorned the Victorian house that the famous neighbor lady called her home. She was furious, and I was so embarrassed. I grabbed my children, and tried to corral the dog that was growing into some kind of a horse, not a canine. Dave pulled up to the house with lunch, and down the road I could see my mom coming. I thought she must have been on her lunch break. She drove an old green truck, mostly rust that was not a model T, but definitely a classic. It was all she could afford and it got her around. I could hear her shifting gears. As the neighbors stared, she pulled that old clunker up on the wrong side of the street with the driver's door right up to the sidewalk! She jumped out of her truck and ran up the sidewalk with an envelope. She had a bonus check of over eight hundred dollars, and she was qualified for a free car! "What? How did that happen?" I wondered.

Although we hadn't been working on our own personal lines, we had helped a lot of others in the previous months. Mom got in prior to the farmers from Holyrood that were going crazy in this business. Craig Mog was a prison guard in Ellsworth, and they also farmed. He and his wife Deb had spilled under my mother, and her check was big! She was so excited. She said she might never clean a house again. I cried and cried and wondered if I was just pregnant and emotional, or if my dreams were coming true. This was really happening! Our check was not in the mail, but I was hoping we had some good news with an arrival today.

Our mail came later in the afternoon. The FedEx truck came before the mailman and he had an envelope for Dave. Dave signed it thinking it was probably from Bert. Dave and Bert would FedEx checks to each other to float the money for furniture until it was delivered to all the stores and the inventory could be paid for. It wasn't anything for them to pick up a load of furniture for $45,000, write a check with a balance of half that, then trade checks and inventory on a dead run for three days, trying to get the furniture delivered and all the money collected before the check hit the bank. I didn't open the envelope. I waited for Dave. He opened it over lunch, and to our surprise it was not only our check from the company, but a letter that said, "Congratulations! Go pick out the car of your dreams, and we will pay for it. Send us the payment booklet, and we will make the payments! We cannot wait to start making your monthly payments and reward you for your commitment to building this company." I freaked out! I absolutely freaked out!

That day we got in the car, pregnant and all, and drove four hours to find a dealer with the exact car we took our picture by just two months ago in Chicago. We drove off the lot in a brand new Q45 Infinity with the gold package. The leather had such a strong smell it was hard to breathe, and the kids fit right in the back seat although I was scared to death to strap their car seats on the leather. The clock in the dash looked like a Rolex. It was so shiny it would blind you if you stood back and looked at it. We took our picture, and we actually had someone video us getting our free car! The car salesman thought we were crazy and believe it or not, he didn't know if he was interested. I didn't stop there. I gave a video to everyone else at the dealership, and a young lady who had just started working there agreed to come to the Kansas City meeting next week. We drove home, and I couldn't wait to hear the comments of our dream stealers now. I guess my little brother would see me get a car yet! Dave and I had a friend drive our car back to Russell so we could ride together. They were friends of ours who were in the business, and now they were ready to get going. We parked that baby right out front! I figured people probably thought the mafia was there now since it was black and had more gold on it than most people had in their possession. Pure class! That's what it was, and it was free!

Meetings were a lot more fun to drive to now. Although we had no idea how we would put a tag on it or pay the insurance for this month, the car was free! We were in high gear. Our checks began to grow, because we were growing. We worked with our group and continued to personally sponsor people. We had two people close to breaking at the leadership level, and one of them was interested in going on the cruise. The company had a promotion to sign up for the cruise if you went Platinum that month, and believe it or not, we had two people get the job done.

The first girl we sponsored was making over two thousand a month by Christmas, but with all of the rumors, she didn't dare build the business! She was scared it was going to go away, and so she was waiting. Each day when I saw her it was like I wanted to beat her, because she wouldn't do it. If she had sponsored four people, her checks could have been four or five thousand dollars. Because it was a business that could be sold, an older couple from Hays, Kansas decided to buy that position from her. They purchased it for about ten thousand dollars. She sold a residual income that was twenty percent of that per month for a one time pay off, just to be safe. I was hurt, and I hated to see my friend quit the business. I called a lady from South Dakota, who I had met at convention, and she took time to counsel with me, telling me she totally understood. She was becoming one of my best friends in a long distance phone relationship, along with a daily tape I could plug in and listen to when I couldn't get through to her on the phone. She was my rock, and whatever she told me to do, I would do. Talking to her gave me a boost of energy. As I listened to her, I dreamed of being a speaker like her someday. I started to acclaim her to our whole group, and they, too, would listen to her tapes and plug into her calls and meetings if they were in the area. She explained to me that sometimes this business is just not for everyone and it's all about timing. She encouraged me not to burn any bridges, because sometimes people come back around. Her own family had done similar things to her, and she realized that I doubted myself. She didn't let me stay down for long.

I told her I was pregnant, and she and her husband offered to come to Kansas to do some meetings. We were really excited to have a famous person who was about twenty levels above us offer to come to Russell to meet our group and do a meeting. By the time they came to do a meeting, we were Two Stars and were working our way to the top. She was amazed that we could live on so little, and yet we never make any excuse to not attend an event or meeting.

After their visit to Kansas, a call came from Chicago. It was KT calling from his office in Chicago for Dave. He wasn't actually on the phone, but his assistant asked if Dave could fly to South Dakota to do training for the top leaders in the company. "Now, wait a minute. Why Dave and not me?" I thought. Dave, with all expenses paid, left on a plane out of Wichita, Kansas without me, to speak to a group in Sioux Falls, South Dakota. Many top leaders lived in this state, and many of them were great speakers. Dave wasn't a big conversationalist, and the trainings we had done for our group were fairly small. What was the purpose of this meeting? Obviously there was a reason they chose Dave, but there was no explanation. Dave was so nervous, he called every thirty minutes. He hadn't even met most of the people, and some of them were the people we had bought cases of videos from who had made sixty or seventy thousand dollars their first few months in the business. Boy, didn't we feel special with our checks that were stuck at four-thousand dollars for six months. Compared to them we thought of ourselves as failures. Self-esteem was not something that was running high for us.

Dave met the top leaders and trained that Saturday on the basics. He told our story and did the eight steps we had been taught at the beginning of our business. He had learned the steps well enough to teach and he didn't use his notes. It was a way of life for us:

Eight Steps:
1. Define your dream with a burning desire for its achievement
2. Make a commitment
3. Use the products
4. Make a list
5. Show the plan
6. Follow up and follow through
7. Start the training process
8. Teach the training process

If you were struggling in your business, it was easy to find out what was wrong. All you had to do was look at the steps and see which one you were missing. There was a work flow that we followed and taught to everyone we sponsored. It was not a new theory. In fact, I had learned it in high school while I was in the first company I joined, and it had been around for fifty years:

1. Find a prospect
2. Show them the plan
3. Follow up with them
4. Start them out right

Dave's training had a lot of bull-riding stories and the lessons we had learned along the way. I think his funniest story was the question he would ask the crowd at every meeting: "Do you know how to tell when a bull rider has lost all of his marbles? Fill his mouth full of marbles, and each time he falls off, spit out one marble. When he had fallen off enough times and his mouth is empty, he has lost all of his marbles!"

Everyone would laugh at his humble humor and his blue-jean ego. Within a few moments of his speaking, the leaders saw his real passion and belief that anyone could do this business. The leaders in South Dakota must have been shocked to see a new kid on the block building a business breaking Platinums like he was, with such little experience and no credibility at all.

We were definitely making a reputation for ourselves. We were called *"The Kids from the Heartland"* and me, I was the pregnant lady with the red hair that cried every time she got up for recognition.

Christmas came and went and we packed for the cruise that was coming next month. I was growing and looking very pregnant, and the bigger I got, the tighter my clothes grew. I wished I could buy some maternity clothes that looked a little bit more professional; but for now, I just wrapped that suit jacket around my men's extra large black T-shirt. I could find economical ways to make anything look a little more professional. Besides that, there were new people at each meeting who didn't know I wore the same suit every night. I had gotten a couple of cute outfits for Christmas to wear on the cruise, and I could not wait. Dave and I had never been to the ocean.

Our leaders were envious, and we assured them we would all be on the next one together. Dave and I packed the kids' suitcases for four days and five nights as we put their little blankets and teddy bears in the bags and headed off to Nana's house. Our moms agreed to take turns watching the kids, switching off days and nights, so they might get some rest in between.

We drove to the airport in Wichita and parked our new free car as far out in the parking lot as we could. I was out of breath just walking to the terminal. I couldn't imagine that my physician had given me permission to get on a plane. I missed the "You Can't Go" rule by about two weeks. Thank goodness I was able to take the trip! We landed in Miami and found our friends at the hotel that was located along the beach. The ship was bigger than a football field, and it had more people boarding it than we had in our entire home town. The people were from all over the world, and I was in awe just looking at all of the different people. I will never forget the chick on roller blades wearing her thong as she skated down the sidewalk along the Miami shore. We were definitely not in Kansas anymore! You could tell the people who were on the ship with our company, because many had their boom boxes packed with their luggage in order to listen to tapes on the cruise. There was no way we could go four days without our tapes and our books ... they were so good.

With the ship departing at four in the afternoon, we had a lot of time on the strip to see the homes, the boats, and the yachts that people in Florida had right in the bay where our ship would soon set sail. I took lots of pictures when they mentioned that Gloria Estafan and Sylvester Stallone were just a couple of the homeowners in this neighborhood. Wow! I dreamed of owning a small fishing boat, and some of these boats cost over one million dollars. I needed to enlarge my vision if I was going to hang out with people like the ones in this neighborhood. One of the top money earners had driven his yacht to the Florida coast all the way from Minnesota, and he planned to be on this cruise with us. We were hanging out with people that made more money in a month than anyone in our home town could generate in an entire year, other than those who had inherited oil wells back when the oil prices were high. There was a lot of old money in Russell, but not many self-made success stories at this time.

We had to laugh as we stood at the rail of this ship, looking down seven stories to the sandy beaches. "Those are the beaches," Dave said, "I told you he would see us on the beaches of the world." I wasn't laughing anymore! I was sure Dave would never let me hear the end of it, and I was thankful he reminded me of my pessimistic attitude at the beginning. That made it a lot easier for me to relate to all of the people I was working with who were married to the biggest dream stealer they had. I used to be one, and now I was learning just how this industry of network marketing really could work, even for a broke bull rider and a beautician.

16

Miles from Home, Decisions Were Made

WE SAILED TO THE BAHAMAS and spent the day on the beach with our leaders. We walked around the ship hoping to get close to one of the people we listened to on a monthly basis but hadn't had the opportunity to meet yet. We did get a chance to meet our mentors from South Dakota, and they asked us to come down to the comedy show later that night.

Dave and I played in the casino, but we didn't have much to lose. It was no surprise that I was out of my allowance within the first few minutes, but one of our friends from South Dakota was winning like crazy. Dave took a seat by him and within a couple of spins, Dave had won over $400.00 in quarters! I was so excited that I took the bucket, cashed it in, and tried to get him to leave while we were ahead. That was enough to pay one payment to Sears or perhaps buy a new stroller for three!

The shows were amazing on that ship, and the dancers had me dreaming of being a ballerina again someday. I had taken some time off from teaching. Now with a third baby on the way, there wasn't much point in having another dance enrollment, but I hoped that Brooklyn would dance.

The three days went fast. We were anxious to see our babies, but hated to leave our friends and go back home. Some of our friends from Kansas were on the cruise with us and had been seated with us each night at dinner. We had big plans for Kansas when we got home!

I took a lot of pictures while we were in the Bahamas and sent postcards to all of my family and friends. One morning during the meeting on the ship we got to hear from our mentor, KT. I sat quietly waiting in the front row for the meeting to begin. I bought over fifty postcards to send to our group back home. I had to refrain myself from sending a few of our critics a card with half of the picture torn off that read, "We're in the Bahamas! Guess you didn't get the whole picture!" I decided to be kind and forgiving instead of getting even with them with my own list of paybacks. I had almost finished writing all fifty of the cards when I looked up, and there he was. The top guy was reading my postcards! I had written to each one of my personals, "I can't wait to get home and help you build your business. I want to help you go platinum!" With a smile, he looked down at me and said, "This is the biggest favor I can do for you." He tore my postcards in half and offered to buy me some new ones. He warned me not to write, "I can't wait to get home and help you." I was somewhat embarrassed. He didn't even apologize, but he gave me some valuable advice. He suggested, "How about, 'You can do it!' Wouldn't that make them feel more confident in themselves than waiting for you to be the source of their momentum and success? You want duplication in your group, don't you? Let's get you some new postcards and give them the message that says that you wish they were here and you know they can do it." That is exactly what I did. I started over, but not during the meeting.

I took a lot of notes. Once again, it was like he was inside of our house. He mentioned there was a difference in hitting the pin level and solidifying the pin level. We realized that we were barely Two Stars and some of our leaders were always in and out of qualification for their pin levels. We needed them to be solid and have more than they needed to qualify to insure they weren't on the verge of falling in and out. In order for us to stay qualified as Two-Stars those Platinums had to be committed to staying Platinum. It was taught to us as if this was a commitment to our upline as much as it was a commitment to ourselves. The advice to the leaders was to sponsor fifteen if you need ten. That way you know you are solid. Don't think you have ever arrived in this business, because it is always a matter of getting a bigger dream and setting a new goal.

Some of the top leaders were not on the cruise, because they had received a gift from the top leader to attend the Super Bowl, with seats on the fifty-yard line. He congratulated the absent leaders on all of their success as their group, who was on the ship, cheered for their mentors. We finished the meeting and had a whole new set of objectives, knowing our work ahead would be like that of the first ninety days. I had two months and two weeks until the baby would be here. I was so anxious to get home that I went to the room and packed early.

We got to the Miami Airport and said all of our goodbyes as we boarded a plane to Chicago. In Chicago we ran to our gate to see if our flight was on time, and it was delayed. We sat waiting patiently as we phoned home with severe home-sickness for those babies. I felt like the first time I had stayed overnight at a friend's house. I couldn't wait to get home and hold them in my arms.

It was good for Dave and me to have some quiet time together. We hadn't had much rest and relaxation for about a year. The cruise was a lot of fun, and what a beach babe I was in my maternity suit, my sunscreen, and my visor protecting my fair skin from blisters on my nose. Now it was cold in Chicago and soon we would be back to reality and back to work of course.

Dave was not excited to see that they had cancelled our flight from Chicago due to a snowstorm in Kansas. In fact, there was only one flight in to the entire state. This flight would arrive in Kansas City at midnight, but our car was at an airport three hours across the state from Kansas City.

We did have some extra money left from the cruise, and for a fifty dollar change fee we could change our flight. It was better than sleeping on the Chicago airport floor. We walked to a lounge to pass the eight-hour wait for the Kansas City departure, hoping that it would not be cancelled prior to the time we took off. At the club in the airport there was a lot of commotion and people laughing, people talking and many were people who we recognized from the ship. I looked up and there was our South Dakota bunch of friends, along with so many people we had not yet met. What a coincidence! Dave and I sat down at a table with a couch, and they all gathered around making us feel welcome and asking us what time we would be leaving. We spent the next six hours talking to people who made over forty thousand dollars per month. That was the best part of the entire trip! Thank goodness we were stranded. We learned so much from them we almost forgot about our flight being cancelled.

We did get into Kansas City at about midnight. Dave called a friend of ours in Russell to see if he was up and told him of our dilemma. I don't know another business where you make friends that are this committed to one another, but at four in the morning our Russell friends pulled into Kansas City to pick us up and take us home.

We got home to the kids, and I immediately started booking appointments and setting meetings. Our goal was to be a 4-Star by the event at Lake of the Ozarks in the summer. I had no idea how it would happen, but I focused on the basics and continued to pursue new personally sponsored friends. We experienced a lot of growth in the groups we had sponsored, and I even invited the guy who measured for our new carpet to come to a meeting. I had to get some carpet before the new baby was born! How could I lay a newborn on this filthy wooden floor that had carpet glue and old tiles stuck to it?

The carpet guy didn't show up at our meeting, but I drove to Great Bend and did a meeting for the people who were in the company. I had invited nine people to the meeting and only one of them came. I sponsored the daughter of the boss who had moved us home from Wyoming, and being a single mom, she was excited to get an additional check coming in. Every day I added people to my list, and in the evenings we drove to do a one-on-one or an open meeting. I had about two weeks left until this baby would be born, and then I hoped to take a week or two off.

In order to be fully qualified, May was the deadline for pin levels that would be recognized in August at convention. If I didn't hit it by this month, how would I do it with a new baby? We worked as hard as we could, but to our disappointment nobody seemed to want it for themselves quite as badly as we wanted it for them.

In April we sponsored a couple of out-of-state people, which was good, but I could not get there to join them and create a sponsoring frenzy before the fifteenth. I explained to them that Dave would come, and he booked meetings in their areas to get them started right within their first month.

Dave took off for Nashville with over twenty commitments of leads that we had called, and they were all going to meet him over the weekend. He drove our car and another couple went out two days earlier to do some meetings prior to his arrival. I sponsored my cousin over the phone from Nashville, and she thought she could get some people together to attend Dave's meetings also. We had groups going crazy in Kansas and we thought we would start some other groups out of state. We needed someone new to break the pin level so we could hit our goal of being 4-Star.

Dave drove the fifteen hours to Tennessee all in one day. When he got there, he rented a hotel suite to hold the meetings. He anticipated a big showing so he made sure he had drinks and food in the room for any new guests. The first day he was so excited. He called me several times. I didn't hear from him for most of the afternoon, but I was sure people were there and going crazy. That night when Dave called he said the couple from Russell had just left his room. They were a bit disappointed, and so was Dave, because none of their appointments had showed up for the meeting. Also, not one of the leads that I had talked to, who were just sure they could make it, came either. I could tell Dave was exhausted and mentally drained. I tried to encourage him, but I realized that it wasn't going to do much good no matter what I said. This was a hard lesson learned.

The next day would be a new day, and he greeted the day with optimism as he called and said, "Honey, I hope we have enough chairs here. This room might fill up today!" I could tell he was laughing to keep from crying, and I agreed that we would surely have some applications from new people today. I tried to call all of my leads, but of course, an answering machine or a kid with an excuse was all I had to show for all of the commitments. My own cousin called and said she couldn't make it to Dave's meeting. She said her baby was sick, and it was a thirty minute drive to the hotel—never mind Dave had driven across five states to get there. Everyone had an excuse, and any excuse would do.

I dreaded this for him, and the drive home would be longer than ever. I hoped that I could get some people to sign up over the phone to ease the feeling of rejection, but I had no luck with our list from Tennessee. The book of the month and two tapes came, and I opened them while I put the kids to bed and prepared for the next morning. I didn't have time to sit down and read, but I knew it would help me if I did.

It was ironic that the book that month's training was called *Acres of Diamonds*. The moral of the story is that some of us sit on a fortune in our own surroundings, looking for the secret bullet or the big hitter far from home, when that next big person is right in our own backyard. There was never a month that I didn't need to hear just what came in the training. I didn't want to tell Dave about the book, but when he called, I agreed with him that we need to build locally first. He admitted he was disappointed, but he was so positive by the time he got home. I guess that is what happens when you have thirty hours to drive and listen to tapes!

From now on, we were focusing on making Kansas our biggest state and on working locally until we had the time and money to burn on trips out of state. I didn't spend too much energy thinking about the money we had spent, the time Dave drove, or the disappointment of the turnout at his meetings. We had to think about tomorrow, because there was nothing we could do about what happened yesterday.

I was glad to see him home, and we put together a new bassinet for our baby that night. Dave's mom had sewn a cover for it with some beautiful lacy material. We washed the blankets and baby clothes that we had just recently packed away. We were anxious for the new little one to be here, and I couldn't help but think of all the things I better get finished before one more little one needed Mommy. The two precious toddlers we had already needed a lot of Mommy. We picked out names and spent the late evening and early morning hours getting ready for the new baby. It was easier to work in the middle of the night while Chance and Brooklyn were sleeping.

17

The Power Is in Promoting

THE DOORBELL WOKE ME UP and I saw someone in a uniform at my door. The dog catcher was at the door with a furry white dog she was trying to contain, and she had two tickets in her hand. One ticket was from last week when we had been gone and another was for this morning. They were tickets for having a dog at large. Our neighbor lady had called the police worried that our dog might get in the yard with her kids. The dog had been running around the block and nobody was watching him. I couldn't imagine how he had gotten out of the seven foot fence. I signed the tickets and then looked at them. There were over three hundred dollars in fines, and I laughed, thinking to myself what a sense of humor God had. I checked the fence as I put the dog back in, and I wasn't surprised to find an escape hole he had dug that was the size of a human. I tried to put some boards on the fence, but I would definitely need Dave to repair it.

The day we packed to go to the hospital I noticed that the neighbor lady had delivered a baby boy and had the blue flag flying that said, "It's a boy!" Of course, it was flying from her newly painted home with tulips poking through newly fertilized grass that was greener than the golf course. Someday, I thought to myself, someday, I will have a yard keeper and the beautiful house of my dreams. For now, I just wanted to fix the fence and repair everything that the dog and the kids had torn up!

Our new carpet arrived and that was a plus, but the carpet guy had every excuse of why he was too busy to make the meeting and too busy to do another business. I let him know that I used to be busy, too, but my way was a lot easier to make ten thousand dollars a month than what he was doing! I had to give him some heat because that he had no-showed me six times in a row at the Great Bend meetings. I asked him to give the video back to me, because I had someone who was serious about making money in Great Bend. I was about to find a key leader there who wanted to get rich. He begged me to let him keep the video and asked if he could bring his wife over next week. I told him I was having a baby on the fifteenth, but the twentieth would be a good night for us. On April 10 Dave and I celebrated our fourth anniversary, and Kali Anne Pitcock was born on April 15. She was over eight pounds and the biggest baby I had delivered yet. Kali was the best baby. She just slept and ate.

My sister's fiancé, Duke, had been through a tough time, and Dave and I had given him a book to read during his difficult time. He was one of the first ones who came to our house, and when he picked up Kali from the bassinet, I could see the difference in him and the impact our caring made on him. It made me feel so good to know that I was in a business where regardless of your past, you could turn your life around. We visited, and he laughed at my tickets on the fridge from the dog he had surprised me with last year. We were sitting in the living room talking about the business and heard quite a commotion outside. Riley, our St. Bernard, had just torn all of the lace tablecloths from the neighbor's clothesline. The lady was on her porch with her broom screaming at him to get out of her yard. I had to get this dog a new pen! I offered the gift that keeps on giving back to the giver, but Duke didn't think he needed such a big dog. I knew I was the talk of the neighborhood, but for the first time in my life, I really did not care about impressing everyone else.

I had to give the dog away that week, and he went to a very good home in the country where he would have room to grow. There was no love lost between the neighbors and Riley, but the dog was a family pet we had grown to love. When the dog stood on his hind legs he was as tall as Dave's brother, and he could pick the kids up and carry them around like luggage. I dreamed of moving to the country and having lots of animals and kids. Someday was surely coming soon.

I measured my life from function to function, always setting new goals and pin levels to reach, and never missing out on an event. The greatest memories I have are the journeys from pin level to pin level and event to the next event. We grew very close to our top leaders, having pot lucks, picnics, and brain-storming sessions, and always recognizing the ones who had done the most. We had traveling trophies and even small incentives we created, like taking them white water rafting for sponsoring eight people. We were starting to see some serious increases in our checks.

The up-coming summer event in Dallas, Texas was one we could drive to in a day. It was eight hours away, and we had about forty people in our group planning to attend. At the event in Dallas an incentive was announced that whoever registered the most people to attend the annual convention in Minneapolis would win a free ticket to convention, a hotel suite, and airfare. The incentive was for that weekend only. I had no idea who I would call and recruit to go. Most of our people with a heartbeat were already in the seats and they did not count for the contest. We were big on winning contests, because it always helped us afford building our business or get to the next event. Our group was growing. We had the title, but we had reached the pin level without the large numbers of people needed to create the volume to make ten thousand dollars a month. Sometimes people reach a pin level, but it takes time to build the residual income that others at that level talk about. One thing we were good at was promoting functions and building leaders. We had stronger friendships in the business than any friendships we had ever built.

I took my list to the pay phone and with a card for long distance; I started calling people at 9:30PM at night. "You have to come with us to Minnesota. We want you to experience this lifestyle. I know you have dreams and want to make this work. We are committed to making that happen with you, but the event will sell out this weekend. We must secure your seat at the national convention! You can always change your mind, but at least give me your information to save a seat!" I promoted the speakers that would be in Minnesota and the recognition they would receive if we got them to the next level. I was focusing more on their dreams and their success than the contest. That is probably why we won. We won the contest with over sixty-five people committed to attend the national convention and to ride a bus from Kansas to Minnesota just three months from then. There were about forty people already with us who had made commitments to go from our group, and I could finally see how this would work if everyone knew what it was like to attend an event. The most downline we had ever had attend a major event was two or three. This was the turning point for us. I knew it! We were taking a bus to Minneapolis! We had three months to get ready for that event. We could be 4-Star by then!

Driving home from Texas, Dave and I used the cell phone for almost nine hours straight. We were in the roam mode and the rates were extremely high, but we knew that the pay off was going to be worth it. We had one bus full, and we were working on chartering a second one. It was still amazing to us that the so-called "dead in the business" people we called from Texas agreed to go to Minneapolis with us on a bus. It must have been divine intervention or the power of our minds. If anyone asked me how I had just done that I would reply with, "I have no idea." I was shocked at my own results. I truly believe that when you are excited, the facts don't count. The tickets were $399.00 per person for the two-day event and the evening meal on Saturday was included.

Many of our leaders had their sites set on the next pin level, and that made it more reasonable for us to set our goals so high. If we could just help them get to Platinum we would automatically hit our goal. We all had charts on the walls, cards with dreams and goals backed up by commitments on visors, mirrors, refrigerators, and even on some toilet seats and bedroom ceilings. We were all going to be rich, and we knew it.

At the age of twenty-three getting rich is really something that you dream about. At the age of thirty-five and forty, many of our leaders just wanted to quit their jobs. In fact, a goal of three thousand dollars a month had them on fire. Some of the older people in our organization wanted to pay off their mortgages or earn a free sports car. In some cases people were trying to earn a new John Deere tractor or a new implement for wheat harvest with their car bonus! Receiving a check for two or three hundred dollars a month was a goal for many of the people we visited. Realizing that a residual check for three hundred dollars a month was more than collecting interest from one hundred thousand dollars sitting in an interest-bearing account, I could see why someone wanting to retire would be motivated by the residual checks. It's tough to create residual income any other way when you truly look at the options. This business might not be easy at first, but getting it started was the hardest part. After that, it would grow for them. We didn't care what their dreams were. We were committed to making their dreams become a reality no matter what it took!

It didn't look like we were going to accomplish our 4-Star goal. However, as winners of the contest, we were invited to the Minneapolis event one day early as honorary 4-Stars. We could hang out with the leaders at 4-Star Club, but the title was not ours. I wanted it so badly I could taste it. Dave and I spent endless hours trying to motivate our groups with the fact that they would get recognized at the convention. All they had to do was fill their circles on the charts with people who wanted more out of life and wanted some great products. We were only four circles shy of achieving our goal. Four people, each with an order, and we would have had it done. We were depending on other people to do things they said they would do, and they didn't get it done.

In life things have a tendency not to happen. You have to be a person that says I am doing this, that's it, period, or you will always fall short of the things you assume will happen. Leaders have to have time to grow, and many of the people we depended on had never even been to an event.

We headed to Minneapolis to our second annual convention. Looking back over the past year or two we had accomplished so much. We had believed that we would be farther along than we were, but I think that is part of the industry. You always want more, because you know what you are capable of achieving.

It was amazing to be in the 4-Star circle! We arrived at a dock where two yachts would take us down the St. Croix River. All of the famous people from the magazines and audio cassettes were on the boat. I dressed in my best pair of khaki shorts and wore a little vest over my white T-shirt. Dave wore his jeans and a polo shirt. That cowboy's legs had never seen the sun, and he was not about to put on a pair of those khaki golfing shorts. That was just not Dave. He was way out of his comfort zone. The yachts were followed by ski boats, racing boats, jet skis, and a lot of other water toys. All of the leaders were enjoying the party as they listened to their favorite music and danced on the top of the yacht. The hot sun was beating down on them and many of them were in their bathing suits and covered with tanning oil. I was as white as an albino goose, and I felt like my freckles were coming out like stars in the night. It was a lot of fun, but it would have been so much more fun if we had brought two or three of our leaders and friends that we knew and loved. We could tell that everyone on the yacht was like family. They were building their future plans together, and they were leaders that had bonded together after sharing many events.

I thought back to the cruise and the way we felt with the friends we were together with there. They would just die if they could have been on this trip. The St. Croix Yacht Club was our dinner stop. Dave and I looked over the menu, automatically focusing on the right side and the prices rather than the food that was listed on the left. There wasn't a single item for less than fifty bucks! I was hoping we weren't paying for our own dinner. If so, the complimentary bread and a cup of soup would have been a stretch. Any kind of seafood imaginable was on the menu, and the people from the city and the east coast were going crazy over lobster, crab, and escargot. Dave leaned over and whispered in my ear, "That's snails, and you know what snails eat—all the poop off the bottom of the ocean!" I had to laugh. There wasn't a rib eye or a fried chicken dinner on the list. We were definitely entering a new territory. We felt out of place, but had to find something to order. Dave and I settled for quail and it was very good. We would hunt for quail in Kansas, but usually we cooked it in a deep fat fryer. This was baked with a dark wine and had relishes adorning it on the plate. The dessert was Dave's favorite part, and I gave him mine to make sure he got full. Plus, giving away my dessert helped me work on that after-baby belly I was still carrying around.

As we got back on the boat, there were stars in the sky and lights lining the boardwalk. It was like we had just stepped into a dream land somewhere. Couples danced on the top deck under the stars of what felt like our house on a float. I had no idea who the singer was they were listening to, but they all loved the music. We were definitely the youngest couple on the boat; and as everyone talked with us, they referred to us as the kids. The only song we knew was *Mony Mony,* and I finally asked them who the guy was singing all of the slow songs. "Frankie! You don't know Frankie?" It was Frank Sinatra they were dancing to, and Dave and I gave them all heck about being old.

At the end of the river trip people began to tell one another good night. This was the end of our 4-Star incentive trip, and the next day the convention would kick off.

A couple from Florida that we knew was congratulating us on all of our success. She wished us well and reminisced about the first time she had met us in Kansas City at a meeting she had flown in to do. We were there when I was first pregnant and we were recognized as new Platinums. I remembered it was her son's birthday, and she had called home from the meeting to talk with him. She was so committed to building the company that they had decided to celebrate his birthday the following day when she flew home. They were going to Disney World! Some birthday! I couldn't wait to do that for my kids.

After all of our recollections of that meeting several months back, she hugged us and said, "It was fun having you join our group this evening. We are going to miss you guys at the next one!" I was confused. Would we not be invited? In our minds, we were already 4-Stars. Then I realized they didn't know just how much our group had grown. They thought we just won a contest.

We took our picture with all of our new friends outside of the Yacht Club, and then we went in a limo back to the hotel. We arrived at the luxury hotel in our long stretch limo. There were distributors standing outside taking pictures like the movie awards were about to happen. I felt like a celebrity, and knew I could get used to the limo and the yacht. We might have to work on the menu; but other than that, we had a great time on the St. Croix River.

As we entered the hotel, I noticed that there were people crowding around the televisions; but we had made it a habit not to participate in watching the news, so I did not ask what was going on. Our theory was that if it was national news that we needed to be aware of, it wouldn't take us long to find out. I went back to the room and began to call our friends that were just a circle or two short. I was not going to be missed on the next 4-Star celebration.

The bus from Kansas, with over seventy of our people heading to convention, was about four hours from the hotel. Many others had driven or flown to Minneapolis, but the bus was definitely the happening place when I called. We made arrangements for those who needed to sponsor someone to meet in our room at ten o'clock that evening. We would be on the phones, no matter what time it was. I was going to work with them until they had someone sponsored. Even if it wasn't official, we would do what we had to do to hit our goal. We had twenty-four hours until our recognition.

Les Brown was in the hotel, along with Barbara Bush, who would be speaking the next night. I couldn't imagine what it would be like to be backstage with the top leaders and meet the speakers on the itinerary. Gerda Kline was a holocaust survivor, and she would tell her story of survival and achieving your dreams in spite of your past. It was definitely going to be a great weekend. There were ten thousand people attending this event!

There was a knock at our door, and it was our friends from South Dakota. They were so excited that we had joined them as honorary 4-Stars. We sat up talking and counseling with them about our business until the bus arrived. Some of the advice they gave us was just what we needed. Their advice included taking our focus off of trying to save everyone and spending our time on personally enrolling new people to create new groups, which would solve the issue of our bonus checks being stuck. They were worried about us financially, and wanted us to get our checks up to where theirs were. I knew it would happen, but how could I stop supporting the "people in depth"? Those relationships that we had built so deep down in our organization were very valuable to me. Not only were they committed to the business, but the people above them were all getting paid commissions based on the work we were doing, which meant the people above them would never quit. Depth was what made it stable, and it guaranteed everyone else's checks above would go up. In most companies the statistics showed that the average group would have 50% coming into the business and 50% going inactive each year. That was not the case in the Pitcock organization. Our attrition rate was the lowest of any group in the entire company, and the marketing vice president had mentioned several times how impressed the company was that our people didn't quit. We had about two or three percent attrition, and we attributed that to working with each person, regardless of where they were. To us it wasn't about how much the check was for us, but how many people in our organization were earning commission checks. If they were a dozen people below us and they called for help, we found a leader between us and them to plug them into, or we helped them ourselves if there wasn't one committed to building the business.

It was midnight when we got on the phone and California was about the only place I felt safe calling at that hour because of the time difference. We were helping people with their lists as we called the West coast prospects, and even some from Kansas where it was just eleven o'clock. It was early morning when we finished, and there was nobody at the office in Houston where our company headquarters was located, but we faxed the applications in anyway. It was the last day of the month, and it was midnight. But we made it—We were now 4-Stars!

It was August 31, just one year from attending our first event. We had moved from the far-back row with only two people in our group attending the event, to a front seat with 4-Star reserved seating and a bus and cars full of over a hundred people attending this event. We had forgotten about all of the people who had said "no" and we really didn't even care about the naysayers in Russell. We had done it!

It felt good to win, and the interview we had the following day was recorded and put in the training on our first training CD called, "It feels good to win!" The event was history in the making. It was full of emotion, enthusiasm, and some of the most outstanding speakers I had ever heard. During 4-Star recognition the company allowed us to come on stage, but our pin level wasn't official so we did not get to touch the microphone. We just stood with all of the others. For me, that was recognition enough. Our group saw us do it. Now, we could convince them that they could do it, too.

There was a moment of silence the next day for Princess Diana who had died in a fatal car accident the night before. Gerda Kline spoke of how she escaped the gas chambers during the Holocaust and rode out of the camp in a truck full of dead bodies. Les Brown told his story and this time it hit me with all new angles. Barbara Bush talked about her family, their cabin, and all of her grandkids and children.

I dreamed of the life that Dave and I would share and all of the things our children would see. I missed my babies more than ever, but I was sacrificing this time away from them in order to give them a life that was not mediocre or average at best. We would live an extraordinary life. I had never seen ten thousand people stand and hold hands to sing "God Bless America," and it was very moving and made me proud to live in a country that allowed us to experience freedom in every way. There was no way to explain what we had experienced. The weekend was "life changing." Where else could you make friends who were happy for your success and not worried that you might pass them on your way to the top? I had never been in a coliseum full of people who were all positive about their futures and had nothing but positive things to say. I wished I could take some of these people back to Russell and get them to move into my neighborhood just to see what it would be like to spend each day with people who were happy, instead of with what Dave called the Russell scowl. We would laugh as we drove past people who looked like they were weaned off of a dill pickle. It was sad that everyone couldn't have the feeling we had in our hearts, but it was because of choices that we had made. There were a lot of people in the same place at the same time we were, and they had chosen not to take action with an opportunity that could change their lives. Now they would either say we just got lucky or convince themselves that it was too good to be true, and that it was just a facade.

Dave and I had come to the realization that we had friends, and then we had true friends. Some of the people who we thought were our true friends had turned their backs on us at the first sign of adversity. We did not need friends that badly. We had each other, and we knew that together we were the only two that really mattered. We focused on what was best for our future and our children, instead of what other people thought we should do. I encourage other people to do just that. Quit listening to what your family, your neighbors, and everyone around you think that you should do, and take a leap of faith to accomplish your dreams. You only live once. Don't spend the next twenty five years of your life doing something that you hate every day of your life while you are surrounded by people you don't like to be around.

We had made new friends from Atlanta, Minnesota, California, and all over the world. Many of them wanted us to come and speak to their groups. There was one couple from Texas who were both chiropractors and who had adopted several children. They invited us to bring our kids and come next month to sleep at their home, swim in their pool, and teach their people how we worked on the phone. How flattering it was to be invited. We were nervous, but we said yes. Dallas was close enough that we could drive.

<u>18</u>

Face Your Fear,
and Do It Anyway

DAVE HAD DRIVEN TO A TOWN NEAR WICHITA to do a home meeting for a brand new couple. We had a couple of new groups that were growing really fast and some that were just a little stagnant. We knew we needed to get some new blood. I was at home making calls and came across a number I had gotten from a friend. It was a phone number of my old boss who owned a convenience store in Russell. During my four years of high school I worked weekends at the local convenience store when I wasn't waitressing at two restaurants. The manager of the convenience store was always a bit intimidating, but he depended on me a lot when he traveled out of town and had always seemed pleased with me as an employee. He had moved and now lived in Manhattan, Kansas, which is K-State territory. I hadn't seen him since 1989 and I thought of him as very successful. With his dark hair and moustache, he was quite intimidating to the employees when he would come to inspect the stores. He was a nice guy, but I was scared to death to call him.

I picked up the phone that evening at about 7:30. Although I wanted to hang up before they answered, I told myself I was more mature than that. I wanted to pray, but his wife answered too quickly. The woman who answered was very nice. I had never met her, but she told me about their twin girls and the fact that they made an incredible income. She was at home with the twins while her husband was gone ninety days at a time on an off-shore drilling rig. I told her about my children as she talked about hers, and we really hit it off. I set the meeting at their house for the following night and couldn't wait for Dave to get home from his meeting so I could tell him the news.

Shortly after I finished making calls, I received a phone call from California. It was a guy we had met in Montana at the first rally where we were presenters. He seemed a little bit nervous as he talked and asked if Dave was home. He said it was important that we call him back when both of us were together. Then the phone rang off the hook with all of our friends who were top leaders. The lady from South Dakota I had followed from day one made the call that totally rocked our world. She was quite upset when she began to talk about of all the problems that our upline had caused the company. I realized the company had faced scrutiny and since it was publicly traded, there had been some trouble caused by negative press; but I had no idea how serious things really were. The company had terminated the top money earner. He was on every video we showed, and we had built him up in a way that I had no idea what effect this would have on our business. I thought my world was falling apart, and I called Dave in the middle of his presentation and told them it was an emergency. I have no idea how he finished the meeting, but he said it was the longest two-hour drive home of his entire life. We were so scared. We feared that our people would scatter in fear.

Know that the industry of network marketing has people that come and go, but the strong relationships built by "you" will keep your business strong.

Thank goodness we had built close relationships with our entire group, because this news was very negative and an ounce of doubt in their minds could sink the ship. There had to be an explanation. We tried to call his office, but there was no answer. This man was Dave's mentor and to Dave he was the reason why he had grown to be such a successful distributor. He was present in every tape, every event, every contest—it was his passion that was driving this company. How could we do it without him?

I was crying, and so were all of the leaders that called our house. The explanation that we received was that he tried to buy the company and tried to force them to sell. If they didn't he said he would leave. In the end he was definitely leaving. In fact he was gone. There was a conference call late that evening, and the president of the company called to let us know that we would be fine if we just stood strong as leaders with our groups. We were committed to standing strong with our group and doing what was best for the company, but we were so sad to see the end of a relationship with that distributor as our upline. It felt like the death of a dream.

We had planned to spend the rest of our lives with some of these people, and they were not all standing strong. In fact, they began scattering to other companies and trying to tear other people's organizations apart in a desperate fight to build a group of distributors to save their incomes. Many were jumping to other deals, and then some were flocking together to protest and argue with the president of the company on the action that had been taken. I was sad, and there was good and bad to both sides of the story; but Dave and I did not have time for all of the politics and gossip. We were getting together to unite with our group and do what we could do to keep things together for our organization and the loyal distributors of the entire company. We made a decision to continue to build our business in spite of the shake up. It was not easy. In fact, it felt like we were walking with shoes on the wrong feet as we struggled to share the story and show the plan; but we did the best we could. We had no other choice. Our organization depended on our leadership, and we had to do what we felt in our heart was right. We were with this company through thick and thin; however, we had no idea how much our loyalty would be put to the test.

I looked around my office at the pictures of friends on my wall. It was heartbreaking, because all of the pictures I had were of those that were leaving the team. I had a dried vase of flowers; my first bouquet when Kali was born was sitting there. The card on the flowers was signed by KT, and now he was gone. I had every name badge from every event, along with the cards and letters of encouragement from so many of these mentors. I did not know if Dave would survive. This was a real blow. Our friends from South Dakota sold their organization to another friend in their group and he became our new upline. His name was Kurt, and he and Dave had met at an event in California back in 1996. We were anxious to get to know him better now that they had sold their organization to him and we were now a large part of his downline. It wasn't long after our South Dakota friends sold their organization that they decided to blanket all of our people with marketing for the new company they had joined. They were doing everything they could to destroy what we had worked so hard to build. I had never seen such greed and so many acts of jealousy and hate as I did with the leaders that battled one another like a bunch of hungry vultures fighting over their prey.

A book I had read early on by a multi-millionaire in this industry said that leaders would lose their vision and sometimes be lured into other ventures by other leaders in the industry. I had no idea it could happen within our company, but I was seeing first hand just what the author called the cardinal sin of network marketing, stealing people from other companies into your downline. I lost all respect for many of the very people who had built my dream and the dreams of those I brought to the events where they had spoken.

When others lose their vision, or your dreams seem faint with adversity you face— persevere and focus on your future. Stay committed to the company you are involved with and don't be easily distracted by other opportunities.

It was a tough year, but we were more committed than ever. We took a two-week trip to Maryland to visit Dave's mom and planned to sponsor people over the phone while we were driving over twenty-two hours on our way there. We toured Washington, D.C. and took the kids out on Deep Creek Lake on a pontoon boat. The rest of the week I spent on my phone, whether we were at the beach, the aquarium, or just hanging out in the beauty of the trees and hills. I loved it there. It was beautiful, but it was hard to build the business with all of the leaders calling and telling me stories of who was doing what and where they were going. I did not care! Dave and I believed you could not shoot two rabbits with one gun, and we were focused on one company with one goal to become the top leader and take them into momentum they had never seen. Fourth of July on the lake was beautiful and we did take some time to relax before the drive home. It was one of the first vacations we had taken that wasn't an event, and the timing could not have been better. We dreamed of returning to D.C. and that area when our kids were old enough to understand the history. They were toddlers, and they were very busy. It was a long drive home with them in the car. We missed Dave's mom and the kids' Nana, but she seemed to be happy in Maryland and was attending college, pursuing a dream of an education in counseling.

I missed my friends and I couldn't believe they were gone. I wasn't sure I was ready to step up and become a top leader in their places. I had a lot of growing still to do. I was working hard to read books and listen to personal development every day. I rode in the back seat of the car with the kids and read *How I Raised Myself from Failure to Success* while we drove to the different sights around the state. I finished two books on that vacation and read Desi's book for a third time on the way home.

19

The Secret of Living Is Giving

WE WERE HOME FOR ABOUT A WEEK and had just enough time to unpack from vacation and pack our meeting clothes. We were booked to do the meeting in Dallas for the doctors we met at the last function. We were flattered that they would ask us to speak at their regional rally and somewhat anxious to meet their organization. It was a windy Kansas summer day and convention was coming up. We knew we should be focused on our goals and personal meetings, but we had this intuition that we were needed to help all of the other leaders and their groups. Loaded down with suitcases and enough movies to keep the kids occupied, we buckled our three little ones in the back of the suburban and headed for Texas. It was about an eight hour drive but it went fast because we talked the whole way. The kids were getting restless by the time we got there. We stopped to let them stretch as we filled up with fuel; but other than one stop, we drove the eight hours straight through.

As we drove into Dallas, I showed Dave the Hyatt where I had attended my first Amway function back in 1987. The top of the Hyatt looked like a golf ball. I remembered being there and seeing a couple named George and Melanie with their three kids on stage. They brought their kids out with them, and I admired her dress and their beautiful family that spent each day together doing whatever they dreamed. Back then, I just dreamed of being successful, but it dawned on me this dream had been in my subconscious mind since high school. There was a time in my life when I gave up on dreams of success and freedom, and now they were the very reason for my waking up each morning. I had to pinch myself to make sure it was real. I had a wonderful husband, three beautiful kids, a business that was growing, and we were going to stay with one of the top money earners in the company who wanted us to train their group. Was it true that if you have a dream and you hold that dream passionately in your mind that eventually you will attract it into your life? It was all starting to make sense to me. I thought I had wasted all those years of failing in that first company, but now I was realizing it was the failures that had led me to this very point in my life. I had grown from every setback in my past. I had looked at those years as wasted and now they seemed as though they were part of the master plan in my life.

We pulled into the suburb of Dallas where our friends lived. It was a gated community with nothing but million dollar homes. There was a long winding drive down to their home. The lights of the driveway lit a path to the circle drive and a beautiful fountain and landscaping. Their gorgeous house was white with red brick on the front and to my delight many pillars. The chandelier was lit, and I could see it through the second story windows. I started warning my kids instantly about their behavior, and Dave and I wondered if we should have gotten a hotel.

We got out of the car and were greeted by our friends as their children came running out with welcome toy bags for all of our kids. Dr. Anne had gone to the party store and made sure that there was a theme for each meal the kids had and a tote bag filled with swim toys for tomorrow and the pool. Wow, I thought, what would it be like to be able to give so freely and put a smile on other kids' faces as they came to visit? The maid took our bags, and we were shown to our room with its own private bath. We ate dinner together as we watched the sun go down on the lake that was beyond the wrought iron fence around the pool. Their house was paid for and they stressed to us that becoming debt free was one of their goals from our age on.

These friends were mentors of ours and I felt like they genuinely cared about us and our future. The kids played until they crashed, and we talked about the things we could do because of the sacrifices we had made. They mentioned that Santa had come to their house in a private helicopter. They had hired him to deliver presents to the kids and had told the kids Santa used the helicopter because his reindeer were busy and the toys were larger items with a special delivery by helicopter.

After their children had celebrated Christmas, they had driven to a Spanish neighborhood and took a U-Haul full of rugs, blankets, mattresses, beds, coats and toys for the kids of the neighborhood. Our friends explained how the children of this poor community had come running down the street to their truck full of gifts as Santa unloaded the items. She and her husband were met by each family as they gave them everything from furniture to food, trying to make a difference in this neighborhood. Their children were able to understand the true meaning of giving and to see how less fortunate families live.

They showed us pictures of a recent trip to Africa where they had met children in need of medical attention. They gave of their time, their services, and the products that our company offered. It was more about what you could give than what you could have.

I was inspired and dreamed of doing the same thing in our home town. Our kids were not spoiled by any means, but we had plenty. We made sacrifices for the freedom we were enjoying. Our kids deserved to be rewarded, but there were so many others who went without. It would be incredible to make such a difference.

We woke up the next morning to a traveling petting zoo, and all of the neighborhood kids ran to the house to hold the boa, the parrot, the hissing cockroach, and any other exotic animal the zoo owner had in his truck. It was amazing to me that people would just have a meal catered with entertainment for a dozen people and not worry about a thing.

The children would be staying with Dr. Anne and their nanny Maria while we hosted the rally downtown at a very nice hotel. Dave and I looked over our notes as we dressed for our training. Hugging the children goodbye, we got into her husband's Mercedes and admired the smell of new leather and the phone that was installed into the dash. He told us the story of how he gave his used one to his mother to surprise her at Christmas. She had never had a luxury car, and it was fun to see her face when she opened the garage. This was like a fairy tale to me. I couldn't imagine giving away so much. Dr. Tom said that he believed your goal should be to give away more than you keep and know that there is more to come, so you never have to worry. It sounded good to us.

We pulled up to the valet parking under the front circle drive of the hotel. The training was packed with people wanting to know our secrets, and there were lines of people wanting to take photos and get our autographs. If they really knew us, they would have known that we were just blue jean kind of people, nothing special, just real people who had a dream and actually worked for it. We talked about the future and where we would all be. We laughed about the people who had told us "no" and all of the adversity we had experienced. It was the adversity that made us so relatable, and the down-to-earth approach we had made it hard for anyone to say no to this business. If we could do it, the people in Dallas were convinced that they could do it.

That night we set a goal with Dr. Tom and Anne that we would both go 5-Star and take the trip to Italy that the company was offering. I agreed to do calls with their group, and Dr. Tom agreed to come and speak to ours. He was not a soft-spoken man. In fact, in most meetings he would raise his voice and holler like an evangelist. He believed very strongly in getting involved and thought those who didn't see it were brain dead. He made a point to tell people that during his meetings. I figured they would either join or run like heck, and that was fine, too.

There were leadership meetings scheduled in two cities, Salt Lake City and Atlanta. The company invited us to speak at both conventions. Salt Lake City was the first meeting and we flew in with all expenses paid, including a limo with our name on a whiteboard welcoming us. There were so many people there we could hardly get through the lobby to our room. Our training was about "How to get your people to join at business builder level and duplicate." Dave and I had more people joining per month than any leader in the company. Although we weren't at the highest pin level yet, we had the fastest growing group worldwide.

Desi Williamson was the keynote speaker and I was a wreck. He spoke of his childhood, and he talked about his grandma and how she changed his life. He mentioned that he was one of eight or nine kids, and of those he was the only one who was not dead from AIDS, drive by shootings or drugs, or was not in prison or on the streets. This man talked about being abused sexually and was very open about his past. I could not imagine that, and here he was on a stage telling his story. My dream was to make something positive out of all of the lessons I had learned and someday tell my story. Maybe this was God's destiny for my life? Desi spoke of his single mom and being home with his younger brothers and sisters a lot helping her out. He ran away from home and lived with his grandma, and she taught him that he could rise above the family tradition of being on the street. She also said he could make something of his life. He did just that, and now people were paying him $10,000 to speak for one hour. I met him backstage and I asked him to sign a book for Dave. Desi's speech had really hit home for us, as he spoke of his brother's alcoholism and the way he loved him so. He talked about how his brother had been influenced by his surroundings, and that it was choices that we all have to make.

Sometimes it was so hard for Dave to see his brother and dad and their struggles. He wished so badly he could help them overcome their alcoholism, but it only caused problems when he voiced his opinion. It was a very emotional evening. We had just heard someone who had hardships way worse than anything we could imagine experiencing, but yet he rose above it all and was changing people's lives.

At dinner that night we sat down at a head table with our name on it. Only eight others could be seated with us, and there was a line of people wanting to meet us. It was very rewarding to see that people were choosing us to be their mentor. The first couple to sit down at our table was from Salt Lake City and they had a new baby in their arms. They talked of how they were inspired by us and could relate to our story. We shared stories and offered business advice. As we got up to leave, they asked what it would take to get us to come to Utah and do a meeting for them. Our kids were close in ages and they offered their home for us to stay. They must have been very persuasive because the next thing I knew Dave had agreed to a thirteen-hour drive one way next month, and it was in his planner. Our family was going to Utah! These people were not even in our organization! We had just met them, but our hearts were so big for the people in this business. We did not ever make decisions based on our benefit. It was all about building the company.

Help enough other people get what they want, and you will have all that you ever dreamed of. It did not say help only the people who you get paid for so you will benefit.

That night we walked downtown. Under the lights of the entire heritage of Salt Lake City, we drank hot chocolate and then went back to our room to get ready for our speech tomorrow. Our friends from Texas were backstage, and we were excited to reunite and see them. It was our job to introduce them during the afternoon.

We spoke to about five hundred people and would do so at another event in two weeks in Atlanta where there would be just as many. The carpet salesman who had no-showed me about seven times had finally joined, and he was in the seats at Salt Lake City. He and his son were getting the big picture and planned to make calls all the way home.

Two weeks later we traveled to Atlanta, and the group from the carpet salesman was growing by about three or four people per day. I spent my days on the cell phone closing whoever he had in his store, and in between he would leave me messages of how many he had sponsored. We had over two hundred new people join that month!

Our checks had increased by seven thousand dollars between August when we attended convention and December. It was approaching the New Year and we believed this would be our best year yet!

I started writing the journals that the book you are reading this very moment is based on and dreaming of the day that I would publish a book just like the one I was reading by Desi Williamson. I had a story, and like everyone in the world who has a story, I didn't want to go to my grave with books unwritten, stories untold, and dreams that were never made a reality. I was starting to realize that our time here was to be spent to serve others and to change people's lives. I was born to do this business!

Looking back over the past few years, we had experienced so many ups and downs, but I was glad we never quit getting up and trying again. The hardest part of success was teaching people to go on faith when they couldn't see that it was happening and getting them to keep doing the right things long enough. All that it really boiled down to was 99 percent mental and 1 percent physical effort. You had to get your mind right or it wouldn't matter how hard you worked.

20

It's Not the Destination—
It's the Journey

KANSAS CITY, MISSOURI WAS OUR DESTINATION in August of 1998. We were downtown at the convention center sitting with a room of people called the President's Advisory Council (PAC). The PAC was an elite group of people who had brought a lot to the company.

Cindy, Dave's mom, had recently remarried, and moved to Maryland to retire with her new husband. Tonight they were in the seats with our kids to see us recognized as the top leaders in the company. Thoughts went through my head about what I would say and how I would feel with so many from our home state in the seats.

We were to introduce Joe Theisman, who was the keynote speaker. Then the next night we would be recognized and speak during the closing session. Cindy and her husband Tom kept the kids all day and then brought them to see us on stage. The kids were four, three, and one and a half years old. Talk about keeping a grandma on her toes; I hoped that she wouldn't be too pooped to come and hear us speak.

It was hard to sleep thinking that tomorrow I would see my ultimate dream come true. I would get to take my children out on stage and become that mentor I dreamed of becoming since I was a teenager. I was the happy wife with her husband and the three kids she dreamed of having. It was almost as exciting as my wedding day! My recognition gown was completely beaded and the girls had matching dresses. Chance's tux was a size two, and he matched his daddy right down to the big black cowboy hat they both wore.

My Journal Entry from August 1998

Three years ago to this date, we were new to the business attending our first event, bankrupt, with two cars repossessed and bills stacked high in the file cabinet. Today we have lived so many of our dreams and are expanding our vision every single day of our lives. Our relationships are incredible, and our family has become our friends in this business. Our picture has replaced the people I used to admire on the cover of the magazine that we got from the company, and our income is that of those we hung around. It is true. You become like the people you hang around with, and you do become the average of your five closest friends.

After the convention, we plan to take Cindy and Tom to the lake on our new 40-foot deck liner which is parked on our street in front of the house with a name across the back that says INCENTIVE. I no longer care what my friends think of my new home-based business, because the things that it has allowed us to experience are beyond my wildest dreams.

Most of my family who joined made over 2,000 dollars per month in this business. Many of them do nothing but buy their products, and I guess that is how residual income is designed to work. As for me, I will never stop working the business because it is my passion and I would do it for free.

It was hard to keep the kids quiet backstage, but watching the energy of the kids from Texas and their parents just ahead of us for recognition, I felt better about how ornery mine were being. I thought back to Dallas, Texas where they had their kids on stage and I had dreamed of taking mine. It all begins with a dream! I had cut their faces out of the magazine and pasted mine and Dave's over theirs so I could look at it every day. I had photos of my kids at their pool with a beautiful lawn and fence, which now had become a reality for us. The dreams that were on our dream board titled, "Dave's silliest dreams" had almost all become a reality. The only thing we had not accomplished was a home in the country on a hill. There was no limit to what could happen, and that is what I wanted to share with the crowd that filled the coliseum.

Dave went out in his bull-riding gear and cowboy hat to introduce Joe Theisman the night before, and now the cowboy and the beautician were about to be introduced as the top producer for the company at the convention. The people from our upline from South Dakota were in the seats, and we had passed most of them in the company, but they were cheering us on as we flew by. The bigger we built it, the better it was for them!

The music was loud, the lights were flashing, and the convention center was on fire. Our names and picture were on the big screen, and the president spoke highly of us as he called out our names, "Dave and Barb Pitcock!" My legs were numb, and I hoped my dress would stay up and I would not trip over the dress that hung to the floor. We entered the stage and then told our story to a crowd that stood on their feet and applauded. There were tears running down cheeks of grown men.

Many of the people in the seats had seen us go from pin level to pin level at each event, knowing that we came from nothing, and that we were truly in love with this business. We were retired at the age of twenty-six and had an income that was more per month than we used to make in a year. It was toward the end of our talk that we took a moment to introduce the three reasons why we had built this business, and as the curtains opened, we introduced them one by one: Brooklyn! Chance! And Kali Anne! They ran to our arms and Chance had on his boots and hat as he jumped into Daddy's arms—arms that were also holding Brooklyn as we walked to the end of the runway parading our pride and joy that drove us to become everything we had become, our children. I believed that this was my "one moment in time."

We had hundreds of people in the seats, and they were all waiting to see what room we would be in for the breakout trainings after the event. We sent the kids to Nana's room and tucked them into bed knowing that we would be up brainstorming until two or three in the morning.

Looking back over the past few years, the excitement of the journey was the very dream that had kept us going to reach this destination. It was kind of like that feeling you have after the new baby is born, or the week after your wedding … you knew it would be this good, but the most exciting part of the venture is the journey to reach your final destination.

Every day in your business is another day of the journey, and you must constantly be setting new goals and reaching for the next level. Never become comfortable and think that you have arrived at your destination. It's the journey that is the sweetest, and that is where you learn and grow from the lessons and the adversity you overcome along the way. The gift that you will be able to give to so many others will be your story of your journey to the top. You will touch so many people's lives when you have overcome the obstacles that were in your way when you continued to break through when most would break down. Never give up, just keep setting a higher mark to reach and dream bigger dreams each time you achieve the one you have been chasing.

21

Don't Be Lured by
the Magic Bullet

I WAS AMAZED to see that some of the people we met from other states were creating all kinds of new tools they believed were the magic bullet. Our group was so focused and the growth we were experiencing was amazing. I couldn't imagine that they needed anything else. There were leaders selling T-shirts and buttons along with books and flip charts. Anything you could dream of, they had it. I was surprised the company would allow these leaders to sell all of their systems at a company function because all of the other organizations were in the house. Dave and I were quite disturbed as the other leaders all tried to get us to buy into their systems that were "new and improved." What happened to the things we had been taught? It seemed as though they were missing some of the training we had been taught by keeping it simple and able to duplicate. People were loading up their credit cards with electronic business cards, CDs, books, and even car magnets with different leaders and their recruiting systems plastered all over them. It was a total disaster, and we knew it was going to be necessary to gather the troops and get back to the basics when we got home. It seemed as though the guy who taught us the simple system had left, and now it was everyone's responsibility to fill his shoes.

Once the animosity began amongst the leaders the events were not as fun to attend. We had won a trip to Italy for two weeks but couldn't imagine the conversations that would take place on that trip in the future. Many of the top leaders had begun to promote their own philosophy to make money on the backside, and it was hurting the company in a big way. People in our group spent more on the tools and systems from other leaders than they had on the entire event. Many of them used the money they had spent as an excuse not ordering their products for the month or making the next meeting. We realized that there were many top leaders working the tools and systems sales harder than the movement of products through the company. We were mad! We made it very clear to the group of leaders that we might be young, and we might be new to this business, but we knew that the best interest of our people was not to max out their credit cards on some system that was supposed to be the next best thing when it would not help them to increase their incomes. We lost a lot of people after that event. In fact, over two hundred people were gone within the next three months.

We stayed home from Italy and focused on keeping our group in unity with the Eight Steps and the simple system we had followed for three years. I was trying to find the good in this, and it was disappointing to think that some of our closest friends were on that trip, and although we had earned it, we had chosen not to go. It wasn't easy to think of leaving our children for fourteen days to travel to Italy on a luxury vacation; and when it came right down to it, I had to believe that we stayed home for a reason. We were focused on building, and no matter what storms came our way, we worked hard to keep our focus. With our mentor gone from the company, and other leaders in the company in charge of the training and system, there was absolute confusion. We weren't very experienced at authoring and reproducing tools, but we had no choice: We had to step up.

We authored our first tape set called "The Formula for Success," and we made a pact that we would not innovate and change or try to fix something that wasn't broken. We were learning that a lot of people in this industry, who have never even built a big organization, try to be the guru who creates a marketing system for people to buy so they can benefit financially from the industry even if they don't know how to create a residual income. I had read a book that talked about this very thing, but I never dreamed it would happen to us. We didn't realize how expensive it would be to produce a training album, but we made a commitment to do what we had to do, and we did it. We launched our CD set, and our group was focused on the basics, which was the same thing we had always taught. We had a barbecue in our backyard, and we built the dream.

Our group was under attack. People got the lists of our downline from other people in our upline, and were calling all of our Kansas leaders with bogus stories and rumors to try to create fear that would cause them to leave our company and follow them. I was glad that we had spent so many evenings in living rooms and so many Sunday afternoons having picnics, potlucks, and inviting our people to the lake, or wherever we could gather with our group. Our group was rock solid, and they were driven more by this adversity than ever before. The good news was we had so many new people that many of them had never met the leaders who were leaving.

We were good and mad, and we hadn't been that driven since we had joined. The dream stealers were back, and this time it was some of the dream builders that we had grown to love. Life is about ups and downs. Some people come and go in your life, and you do not know why. I wrote a letter to our upline that had been terminated from the company, and I mailed it to his office in Chicago. He was someone who had come into our life for a short three years, but he changed our lives forever. Dave and I still missed him and sometimes dreamed of what it would be like to run into him again. What would he think if he could see us now—that broke beautician with the babies and the bull rider?

I had so many questions that were constantly in my mind. I kept wondering why this all had to happen to us, and yet there was no good answer. Why would a leader making over $150,000 a month leave for a better opportunity when so many of us had such faith in him? People said it was a business decision for him. Although we didn't understand it, I had to believe that God had a plan. It was just hard to make sense of it all at a time like this.

22

Tragedy and Triumph

THE NEW MILLENNIUM WAS COMING and many thought it would be the end of the world. Dave and I thought they were all crazy, but 2000 did sound funny after being in the 1900s for twenty-eight years of our lives. People in our group were setting goals like never before, and we were celebrating our best year yet in spite of all the road bumps along the way. New Year's and Christmas were magical with the kids. They were old enough to really get into the holidays and I had seven trees in the house, including one in each of their bedrooms. After closing the store I finally had time to decorate at home. I had all of the trees from the store in my attic and many leftover decorations from the retail displays that hadn't sold. I loved Christmas. To me celebrating was giving all that we could give. It was the greatest feeling in the world. Even when we had very little, Dave and I would make something for everyone just to see them smile! Kali chewed the rest of the paint off the baby in the manger's head as I told the kids about Christmas with my ceramic nativity set! Whether they were old enough to understand or not, it meant so much to me. I loved to read them the stories and celebrate the season.

We were finally on our feet and it was not a struggle to give gifts to everyone. We still had a basement full of Bob Dole T-shirts, and we joked every year that we were going to give them out for Christmas. Now we were laughing about it, when I never would have imagined that it could be funny. We had grown a lot over the past four years, and we no longer struggled. We gave more away than we kept and we entertained our leaders in ways that others could not believe. Just for fun Dave bought our leaders plane tickets to Chicago. We entertained them with limos, suites at the Ritz-Carlton, and dinner at the Signature Room on the 97th floor of the John Hancock building. We were planning our futures together and working hard to be a mentor to them, just like our mentor had helped us build our dreams. We invested in the people in everything we did, knowing that if we would build the people, they would build the business. It was going to be an amazing year indeed.

Kali turned three in April, and Chance would be starting first grade. Big sister was moving on to second grade, and they would both be in school all day. They were really growing fast and it was getting a little bit easier now that they could feed themselves. We didn't have two in bottles and two in diapers or pull ups. I couldn't imagine what it would be like not to have Chance home with Kali for half days. He was her entertainment!

Summer was upon us with our days being spent at the lake or the park, and our nights spent building the business. We had achieved a level in the business that our group had taken a life of its own. I wondered why there were people who would still question if it would work or not; and believe it or not, there were still some of our friends who weren't sure that it was a good deal. We had everything we had dreamed of and were quite comfortable in the business. It was not hard to live on thirty thousand dollars a month in a town like Russell, Kansas. We were starting to think of other things that we could do with the money that would make a difference in other people's lives. I dreamed of opening a camp for young girls—perhaps to help them deal with the trauma of their parents separating or give them encouragement to get through tough times of their teenage years.

I spent my days focusing on my kids and being active in everything they did. Dave was coaching Chance and Brooklyn's tee-ball teams. Chance played for AGCO, the station where Scott, Dave's brother, worked. We would all gather at the ball fields on summer nights. We had certain nights of the week we built the business, and other nights like every Wednesday that we designated just for family. The kids knew when it was "family" night. We would rent movies or have a fun supper at the park or maybe even go to Pizza Hut. It had been years since we could actually go out to eat. It wasn't even worth it when they were all little, because there was always someone getting in trouble or throwing a fit just when it was time to eat our meal.

The kids were at a fun age and our business had taken a life of its own. We planned some vacations. One weekend we actually went to Worlds of Fun for two days and took my brothers and sisters and mom to celebrate Mark's seventeenth birthday. My little brothers and sisters were all growing up, and my mom was starting to get on her feet with a residual income of several thousand dollars a month and growing. We took the weekend and just rode kiddy rides with the kids and watched the dolphin show while the teenagers and mom took advantage of the roller coaster and all the thrill rides of a famous amusement park in Kansas City. It was one of the first vacations my brothers and sisters had ever been on with our mom, who had struggled for so many years. It had been ten years since my dad left and her kids were very small at that time. I had a great time! Our kids had a blast, but we were exhausted after carrying them around the park. We drove home that night from Kansas City.

On July 22 it was hot. It must have been 105 degrees that day. We could see the lights from the ball field from our front porch and hear the announcers as their voices echoed for blocks. It was a calm summer night and the stars were out. I remember the sounds of the air conditioner kicking on constantly, and the cars revving up as they drove past the high school, which was just behind our house. We put the kids in our room where we all snuggled up in our king size bed after our exhausting weekend. We couldn't hear a lot upstairs because the bedroom was on the far end of the hallway. It was an extremely large home that used to be a rest home in the 1900s. We had remodeled it to be a beautiful historical colonial with the main living area downstairs and all of our bedrooms on the second level.

Morning came quickly. It was about 9AM when I heard a knock so hard on the door downstairs; I wondered what could be going on. With our business growing the way it was, there was always someone at the door. We were used to people coming by all the time and our phone never stopped ringing. A visitor waking us up was not anything out of the ordinary. I could not believe we had slept in until 9:00AM, because that didn't normally happen. I got up to get a robe and by that time my mom and my sister Lori were in the house and standing at the foot of our bed. Dave and I were a bit delirious, but it didn't take us long to wake up. I thought it must have been an emergency for them to barge right in. With concerned looks on their faces, they asked if we had heard our phone ring. The phone and answering machine were on the main floor. With the air conditioner running I never heard a single sound. Missing a call would not have normally been that big of a deal, but this time I was sorry I had missed the call.

"Your brother is missing," my mom said, with a look in her eyes I had not seen before. "My brother?" asked Dave. My mom explained to him that she had just seen Dave's dad and although Scott's car was parked just two doors down from our home, he had been missing since last night.

We were up immediately. It was a long twenty four hours. Dave searched every place he could think of along the river, country roads, and any of the places he and Scott normally went. We hoped he had just taken a trip to Mexico to get away from it all, like the one they had planned when they took me to Missouri instead. I was sure that people must be overreacting, but Scott's roommate believed that it was much more serious than a trip.

I called Cindy, Dave's mom, in Maryland, and we had her on a plane within a few hours to be in Kansas City that evening. Dave didn't want to stop searching, but he had to get to the airport. As he left to make it there in time for his mom's arrival, he told me to call him if anything was reported. There was a state-wide search by sheriff's departments with many of his friends looking for evidence of where Scott might be.

When Dave had been gone about an hour, and it seemed forever, I went to the campground to be with my mom, calling every five minutes to his dad's house and the sheriff's department and I called Dave to check on him. I was so worried about his state of mind and making the trip by himself. He had three hours left to drive when I was on the phone with him and noticed a call coming in from his dad. The news was not good, and at that moment I knew our lives would never be the same. They had found both boys, Scott and his friend, and neither one of them was alive. It was suicide, and we were too late. I felt so helpless. There was nothing I could do to ease the pain on the other end of that phone. Dave was half way between us and the airport, and I knew he was completely shocked and devastated. Scott was twenty six years old when he took his life.

I watched his big brother fall apart and there was a piece of him lost that day that would never be replaced. Would he heal? It was so hard to think of the pain he felt on the other end of the phone, and the drive to pick up his mom would be the longest drive of his life. How would he tell her when she got off the plane? I wished I could be there to comfort them or to hold them in my arms. I felt physically sick and I could hardly function to take care of my kids. Regrets and blame were running wild. Feelings of sorrow were there, but with suicide it was more than sadness. It was also pure guilt.

Dave blamed himself so much that when I saw him I wondered if he would survive it. What could we have done? We had taken our kids to an amusement park that day, having no idea that this tragedy would take place around midnight on that Sunday night as we were tucking our kids in bed and snuggling up after a busy weekend.

In all of my life I have never had such sorrow, such regret and such guilt. I believed that there must have been something I could have done. I thought of all of the lunch hours and nights we sat up talking. I thought of the road trips, the holidays, and even the tee-ball games. How could I have changed the way he felt?

I was in shock, and so was our entire town. It was not only Scott who died, but also a friend that was with him. The kids in Russell gathered in a group of over a hundred people that night when Dave got back to town. It was a terrible tragedy, and I had no idea just how bad things were going to be. My kids didn't quite understand what was happening, but they did not see Daddy smile, nor did Nana Cindy show any signs of happiness for what seemed like a long time.

Depression was something I had never seen anyone go through. This went on for months and months until I finally had to make a call to someone to get help so I didn't go crazy. I wished I had been a wife who did not care if my husband went out every single night and partied, not worrying about his family—just so he could have had more time to be around his only brother. A part of me wished I hadn't been so verbal about my beliefs. Scott might have invited us to hang out with them, even though we didn't always fit in with the crowd. For a moment I wanted to trash every single thing I had ever worked for because even my own husband made me feel as if I were "weird" to think a positive thought or dream again. I believed Dave would destroy everything he had built because of his feelings of blame and guilt. In his mind he didn't deserve any happiness, any success, and definitely not financial freedom. He was full of hate and anger that sent each day into a spiral of emotions, and I never knew what would happen. It was almost like walking on eggshells minute by minute. If I tried to make him feel better, it would only start a debate. He would say that obviously, I hadn't lost my little brother, so I had no idea what I was talking about, and my advice did not mean anything to him.

It was over six months before I spoke to people in our downline. I would avoid everyone and hide if they came to the door in fear that they might see my husband in such a state. Leaders began to call and beg me to "get Dave back on the horse." They had no idea how extreme things were and I hoped they would never see this side of him. Dave hated himself. He hated people, he hated material things, and even hated the industry. He wanted to quit every good thing that had ever happened to him, and sometimes I thought he even hated me. As Dave went through his mood swings, our children began to understand that Daddy was sad. They thought he would always be sad, and they would talk to me about why he was mean or mad. He wasn't mean to them, but for the "Daddy" they knew who used to be the highlight of their day to be suddenly gone, was confusing to them. The daddy they saw did not have anything to say, did not have anything he wanted to do, or anywhere he wanted to go. He was like a rock that wouldn't move and I never knew how he would react.

If our people saw Barb Pitcock without Dave, or Barb with the Dave in his lost state, I was sure they would quit. They would doubt that our leadership would never be the same. Dave and I were a team. To build it by myself would be like taking the lead singer out of our favorite band. I compared it to some of the legends who have tried to replace a missing band member with someone new or do it on their own. It is just never the same. I didn't want to be solo! I didn't want to be "Barb Pitcock," but I thought if I could work leads who didn't know me, I could build an income to take care of us. I was sure that with our changed attitude our group would leave. What business would hold together if you were missing for six months and wouldn't even talk to the very people who were there for you?

People from our group were the first to call during the tragedy and the first to bring food. They sent cards, letters, and more flowers than that mortuary had probably ever seen. There were friends from all over the nation who came to our support. Yet we could not find a spark or a slight ember to keep our fire burning, not just for our business, but for our passion and our life.

23

Integrity and Character

MY HEART WAS BREAKING and I was scared. I needed someone to tell me that it would all be okay, but there was nobody I could talk to in our business, and I needed someone I could trust. Out of total desperation I started to look for a leader in another company to help me build an income stream, in case my residual income went away. I could not face my friends to tell them that what used to be so special was not in our hearts. In fact our hearts were empty. I wanted to be passionate, but I was lost without my partner, my friend, and my husband by my side.

I made a call to a woman named Laura Kall who was a mentor of mine who I had read about in many magazines. I never met this lady, but I wanted to grow to be successful like her someday. I thought I would let go of the dreams I had that had died, and start over without telling anyone what I was doing.

Laura Kall was a top producer in another company. I waited for her to answer. I was nervous wondering if she would even talk to me. The lady who answered was her assistant. She took my name and number and gave me a time when I could reach her between appointments, but only for a few minutes. I took my chances and was persistent until I got through. I told her I was a fan of hers who needed a friend. I began to cry uncontrollably to a total stranger begging her to help me start a new business within her company. In most instances a leader who had someone like me call them, knowing what I was capable of, would be excited to enroll me on the spot. Not this woman. She was a true networker who had integrity. She encouraged me to talk as she asked me questions about my business. I explained to her that my dreams were dying and I could hardly function. I looked at my kids, and I didn't want to ever have to go back to work! She assured me that if the relationships I built were strong, the checks would continue to come in. That is exactly what happened, and they grew by several thousand dollars a month. Laura urged me not to leave a company I had built for six years. With complete honesty she said it was not easy to start over, and people should never leave one company and think that they will have their group intact in a new venture. Beliefs are shaken, organizations are torn apart, and the people who you think are strong enough to survive often give up.

I could not imagine ever doing anything that would hurt my group. I had planned to start over on my own with a different story. That way I didn't have to tell my real story without the very person I had existed for also being there. This woman encouraged me in every way. She was building her business without her husband being involved in her business. She was a million dollar earner and said her husband had a business of his own in an area where he was talented. She said he supported her, but there is no way they could build it together. She was the networker. She was booked for conference calls all evening, but she took more than just a few minutes with me. She genuinely cared about my success in the industry. I asked her many questions about her company and she obviously believed in what she was doing. Never once did she have any intention of my becoming a part of her team. She wanted me to believe in myself enough to pursue the dream I had worked so hard with Dave to build.

As I hung up the phone that night, I felt hope. I dreamed of being able to rekindle that spirit I once had. I prayed that I could have as much integrity and love for the industry as a whole as the lady that I had just talked to. That must be why she was a millionaire in her company. She was such an example to me.

I cried, and although I wanted to call my friends in the business, I was ashamed of the condition I was in. I didn't want them to think I was ready to get back to normal, because things were far from normal. I missed them. I wanted to be in communication with them, but I wanted to protect my husband from anyone seeing what he was going through. It was hard to hide. I think most people probably knew, but I worked hard to hide the fact that he was so broken.

To smile would mean that I was not grieving, and then I would feel guilty if someone noticed. To get back to normal might mean that I didn't care about those who were grieving. I just stayed in this rut for months and months until one day we were invited to speak in Orlando at a major event. How could I commit to this? I had no idea what six months from now would bring. How could I say no? After all, my life had been changed by the company, and they needed me to speak at a convention. I felt like I was paralyzed.

The holidays were coming and I just wanted to run away. Our checks continued to come in, and believe it or not, they were growing. The check for November came on December 15. We stood in the foyer and ripped open that FedEx envelope and together we held that check! It was for $17,000, plus we had two free cars that they were paying for! Dave had big plans for this check, and those plans had nothing to do with material possessions. He didn't want any stuff. He just wanted to give everything away. Dave took our check for the month and bought plane tickets, cruise tickets, stockings filled with sunscreen, sunglasses, and goggles for seventeen family members including our moms and all of my brothers and sisters. The holidays were hard, but on that Christmas Eve we made a decision to celebrate life with the people we loved and go far from home to take them to the beaches they had never seen. The trip was planned for February. It was hard to get in the mood to do something like that, but if you could have seen their faces when they opened those stockings, it was worth every penny. My mom had never even flown in an airplane, and soon we would be in Cozumel, Mexico, and the Caribbean.

Network marketing is not about things. It's about freedom—freedom to do what you want, when you want, and to be able to afford it. Freedom to us was spending time with the people we love. On that trip, Dave and I sat on the beaches and watched my brothers and sisters run into the waves of the ocean that they had never seen. It was a dream come true for them, and for us. We could feel good about what we had given. My sister got married on that cruise with all of us there to celebrate. My dad and his new wife were also with us on that cruise ship. After a week at sea and a week with all of our family at Disney World, we spoke in Orlando to over 750 people. Hearing Dave speak with such passion about the power of residual income, I had a glimpse of hope that there was an ember deep down inside him that could eventually grow to be the fire that once had driven him to live each day with happiness.

Dave's speech brought people to their feet in Orlando, and he told the story to those people in the seats who had no idea that such a successful man could feel like such a failure, and yet find the strength to share from his heart. Dave was not a failure. In fact, to many he was a hero. Most people thought Dave was living a life of happiness, but success and happiness is something that you have to feel in your heart. Success is not defined by your finances or your possessions. Success is knowing in your heart that you have a purpose and a passion to live, and it was something Dave lost over that past year.

That night on the stage in the lights did not turn things around completely, but I knew that Dave believed that residual income was a blessing that had allowed him to take a year off. Any other boss or company would have let him go, because he was not producing. The power of residual income had allowed someone who could not find the energy or the strength to get out of bed to increase his income. The passion showed throughout this story, and without a dry eye in the seats, people were making decisions about their lives. They all had a pulse and were breathing, but so many were not truly "living" each day. Life is short and we all have a number of days that we will spend on this earth. Dave's message of building a strong business with relationships and a solid residual income inspired the leaders of that company to take action. There had never been a time before that I saw people rise for a standing ovation that lasted for over ten minutes, and I knew in my heart that someday we would build an organization stronger than ever before.

I was so proud of this man who poured his heart out to a room of total strangers. This was the man I knew and loved. I prayed that he would find the strength to use his potential. I also prayed that he would not let his self-blame bury his dreams for those who were still living—the three children in the front row clapping for their daddy while he was telling his story. They knew the story all too well. They lived with this man, and he was their hero, too.

We never hid anything from our children. We were very honest, and they knew that it was going to be a long road to recovery. We talked about Scott almost every day. Instead of avoiding the fact that Daddy was grieving, the kids realized it was okay and understood that it wasn't them that made him sad, nor was it their fault. I felt like this was important especially in the years to come.

It was amazing how many people would come up to Dave at different events where he spoke and share their experiences. People would share with him things they were currently going through, such as the loss of a child or a sibling, the struggle with their emotions. Or they

talked about the words of encouragement that meant a lot to them when they heard his story. It didn't make it any easier knowing there were people out there who were benefiting from his story. Obviously it didn't take away the feelings of loss or pain that Dave felt, but we could see that he was having an impact on other people through the business and his speaking.

Whether it's the loss of a loved one, the loss of a dream you had, an illness, a financial setback, or even a relationship gone bad, people experience feelings of tragedy on the road we call life. Sometimes it is hard for people to keep moving when they are paralyzed by fear, crippled with anxiety, or just drained from the depression that often creeps in. I am not an expert in dealing with tragedy nor have I experienced some of the pain that others have, but I have been with and observed those who have suffered from these feelings. It seems to me that if you keep your hands and your mind busy and if you surround yourself with people who have some vision and a purpose, it is easier to get through these times. Idle time seems to be the worst enemy for a person who is having a hard time getting through something. I would notice during those first few years that if Dave was busy or involved in a project, reading and listening to encouraging words and surrounded by people who were on a mission with him, it seemed to help. It did not take away the challenges or his feelings of loss, but it was so much better than just sitting and dwelling on the feelings that were so vivid at the time.

Jim Rohn was in our monthly training series that came, and he had a tape on character. He stated that a person with character is someone who follows through long after the excitement that was there in the beginning is gone. I wanted to be a person of character.

I thought back to the call I had made to Laura Kall, and I wanted to send her a letter telling her thank you, you were right, things are going to be okay. Someday, I dreamed, I would be a mentor to many who would look up to me as a person of such integrity as she had shown. I would inspire the masses and make a positive influence on their lives.

24

Freedom at Last

THE CRUISE AND OUR WEEK AT DISNEY WORLD were amazing! This was a dream come true to see Cinderella's castle and feel the excitement of our kids running up to Tigger and Pooh. I was so ready to break out of the rut we had been in, but I still felt like I should be sad or feel guilty if I laughed or smiled. Dave's mom was with us at Disney World, and it seemed like every song in every Disney show we went to was a tear jerker for both of us. Tarzan was my favorite show. Of course, the song at the end had me in tears, but it felt good to cry. Even today, when I hear the song by Phil Collins, "You'll be in my Heart," I can almost smell the cotton candy and the popcorn and feel the warm Florida breeze that was blowing during that song. The trip was magical just like I had always dreamed.

No matter how awesome it was to have worked so hard that I succeeded to the point that we could take our kids and whole family to Disney World, I never expected to also feel an emptiness and loss about Dave. I found myself a bit resentful most days, was sometimes angry, and always wishing that I could turn back the clock. I missed my husband the way he used to be. I had never watched someone go through so many stages, but the lesson that I learned was something that would make me so much stronger. Evidently strength is something God thought I needed to learn.

I developed a compassion for those who had lost a loved one. I understood in a way that I never did before that the pain and feeling of loss doesn't just go away—it takes a long time. When I saw families with their little toddlers walking around laughing and hugging, with no worries in the world, I would wonder how long it would be until we would all laugh and hug and smile again. One minute I would think things were getting better, but then thoughts and memories would creep back and that would send us into a total downward spiral. I never knew when that was going to happen.

I realized that everything that glitters is not gold. A family may appear to have it all, and yet they may be looking for something. People need hope for their future. I knew that I had a vehicle that could have them waking up with passion for the day and excitement about a goal to accomplish. True tragedy is not always death or defeat. Tragedy is when people are still living and their dreams inside of them have died. They live the rest of their lives walking around this earth with a pulse, but with no spirit for life.

I was becoming more and more passionate about helping people enjoy the time they had with the people they love. I believed that I could instill belief into others. I began to write a book, and I dreamed of speaking to audiences, sharing our stories of setbacks and disappointments, and also sharing the results of our hard work and persistence that were our victories.

I made a decision to be the victor, not the victim, and that was not an easy decision. I found it easy to feel sorry for myself every single day, but I hated that feeling. It took effort to find good in everything that happened. I still cannot find good in some things, but I don't ask why bad things happen to good people anymore. I have faith that there is a higher power in charge of my destiny, and it is up to me to make decisions to grow stronger and keep trying. I believe that we can achieve the dreams that God has put into our hearts or he would not have put them there in the first place. My message to others became more about the moments that take your breath away. It was amazing what happened in the next twelve months!

Dave came to me one day and said he wanted us to set a goal to become the top distributor in the company. He believed we had what it took to achieve the company's highest pin level. Only one other distributor had this title, and he had been with the company since 1984. He definitely had more experience than us. I knew we had the work ethic, but sometimes I questioned Dave's idea. It would take exactly double the number of personally sponsored leaders that we currently had, and I would have to be one of Dave's fifteen personals to hit the necessary pin level, in addition to seven others. We had seven solid leaders, and to achieve this we would need fifteen. We had about four months to do it and it was just like Dave to give us ninety days to meet our deadline. That was pretty much the standard way we achieved our success, trying to hit the next pin level before the next function. Why would we want to do this? We did not necessarily need the money. We were comfortable. We definitely didn't need the stress of doubling our organization that had taken five years to build, and, what's more, doing that in ninety days. In spite of this, it sounded like a great goal.

We had grown to love the company and the people at the helm of our company. Dave and I knew that there were a lot of leaders that were basically retired, and we dreamed of taking this company into momentum in a way it had not experienced for several years. Our goal was on a 3 x 5 card. Our posters with circles to be filled were on our office wall, and we were on a full-blown mission.

We met with our top leaders and some of the new people they had sponsored. We shared with them the pin level they could reach by the national convention. We wanted the vision in their minds to be what we could do for them, not what they could do for us. We knew if we could help them find the dreams and goals that stirred their souls and show them a way to achieve them, they would move heaven and earth to make their dreams a reality. There is no other way to motivate a man than to show him the way to achieve what he desires. That was the first step, and that would solidify the seven we had. Then we needed to find seven new ones and help them on their drive to the top. I, plus those seven, would make the eight we needed. How in the world would we take fifteen leaders to the top pin levels in ninety days?

Personally sponsoring new people was the ticket, and showing them that they could be one of our fifteen joining us on the convention stage was motivation for them to get the job done. National convention was scheduled in Nashville, Tennessee in August at the Opryland Hotel. I could just imagine my kids on that stage with us and that was honestly what drove me more than anything else. I was picking out dresses for the girls and a tuxedo for the little man. Our goal was to be solid Presidential Platinum with fifteen of our friends whom we had personally sponsored and helped achieve the Platinum level. This was the top pin level in the company. We must accomplish this by the summer, and spring was on its way.

The work that we did was not different from the basics we learned in 1996. The difference was that we had more experience, a higher belief, and a work ethic like nobody had ever seen. Our leaders did what they saw us do. As a result, more than 400 new people joined our organization each month, at the highest level of enrollment, and it was consistent every single month. Our residual check and our other bonuses more than doubled. I didn't think much about the check, and that was not how I thought it would be. While I had always dreamed of checks of over $40,000 a month, the money wasn't that big of a deal now. The passion for helping others spend time with the people they loved was mostly what we talked about at meetings. Our story was very moving, and we had conviction as we described residual income and what it had meant to us after Scott's death. *Stories sell, and facts only tell.* Remember that when you open your mouth to convince someone to buy a service, a product, or a business opportunity.

Our story would take about half of the meeting, and then describing the way the business worked took the other half. What we could do for them was the focus. When we stated the worst case scenario, people had no reason not to join; but there were still those with no vision who declined to join.

In July we hit the Presidential Platinum level. In order to achieve this highest pin level, we had to double the entire organization we had built over five years, and we had done this within one year. We had twice the number of personally sponsored leaders who had to reach the leadership level. We did it with a simple decision and a new list of people to call.

We planned to take our group to Nashville with us. People were packing vans, cars, busses, and some leaders even set up group discounts on airplanes to get their groups in the seats. Events were the ticket to success. It was not how many people you had in your organization, but how many were with you at the functions. Using an equation to track our progress, we knew it was the people at the events that took our business to the next level. Those who didn't attend the functions were nothing more than product users after six months, and many of those eventually quit.

I used to question myself, wondering, "Why do people quit?" People quit everything. They quit the gym, they quit relationships, their churches, their jobs, and their community groups … people just lose their vision. Why do marriages end? I believe it is the same reason. Couples lose that fire of enthusiasm, the passion for a brighter future, and goals that they share. They become bored or don't believe they can achieve what got them started in the first place. It takes motivation, and it takes effort to stay committed and not quit. It's hard to stay committed on your own. That is why the constant personal growth—learning more, reading more, meeting people who can help you grow, and staying in fellowship with positive people—is so important.

There were so many times when we wanted to quit. We had reasons to justify our quitting, but we didn't. Some days I would feel down and Dave would pull me up. Obviously, sometimes I did the same for him. Who is your mentor? What are your dreams? Who pulls you up when you want to quit? You have to promise yourself you will not quit, making that a priority, no matter what.

Looking back at the timeline of events in our lives, we had peaks and valleys, but always a peak after hitting the lowest of valleys. I am thankful for the things that pulled me out of those valleys, mainly the books and tapes. I am grateful for the mentors I had that instilled faith in me, and believed in me when I did not believe in myself. I know that God wants all of us to have the many experiences, blessings, and freedom that He created for us to enjoy. I do not believe we are on this earth just to pay bills, worry about debt, work two jobs, become overweight, and struggle with relationships because of stress. There is so much out there for each and every one of us. It is our decision to see our opportunities and take advantage of them with the talents, the blessings, and the time that we are blessed with on this earth.

On stage that night in Nashville I could not see with all of the cameras flashing. It was impossible for us to get to our room and change, because the walk from the ballroom to the Presidential Suite was lined with fans of ours who wanted a photo and our autograph. We signed autographs and took pictures for three days straight. At one point of the program, the company's vice president and I were on stage in our casual clothes from the afternoon, and it was the evening session. It was amazing to see how people reacted after hearing our story and the goals that we had accomplished. It was like the four-minute mile that nobody believed could ever be run. The fear was that if you ran a mile in four minutes, your heart would explode. In our industry Dave and I had just run the four-minute mile. Others were lining up with belief that they could do it, too; and we knew that they could.

The Nashville interview we had recorded three years prior to the convention was titled, "How it feels to Win!" That summed up the feelings we had inside. Our convention theme was "Get in the Game." That, too, was a call to action. I am always intrigued by the people who attend the events and get excited but do not go home and take action. Why do people read books, listen to tapes, and continue to learn, but then don't use the skills or advice that is right in front of them? It all comes down to belief and self- esteem. You have to believe that you can do what others have done. Why not you? Why not now? Time is ticking away every day. Our lives are but a blink of an eye, and then we are finished on this earth.

I was already emotional as I clung close to Dave in his arms backstage. This was the night we had dreamed of as we worked so hard during the previous weeks and months. My heart was pounding to the loud music as the lights flashed. I caught a glimpse of those three little Pitcock kids in the front row, standing in their chairs by their Nana. The master of ceremonies welcomed the people, and then after he introduced us and told about all that we had overcome and accomplished, I heard those words, "ladies and gentlemen, here from Russell, Kansas, please help me welcome Presidential Platinums, David and Barb Pitcock!" I think the song playing was "Dreams" by Van Halen, but the only thing I remember is the tears that were falling from my eyes. I couldn't even speak. It took me some time to get my composure as our organization went crazy, just as if we had just won an Olympic Gold Medal.

I was ready when we were introduced on that Nashville stage, as I looked out at the thousands of people in the seats. We had hundreds that had come from Kansas and by now our group had grown in many of the other fifty states as well. I wanted to share our success story, and I wanted that audience to know that they could achieve something, too. I truly felt like anybody in the seats could do what we had done, and even more, if they would try. The key words are, "If they would." Dave and I had worked hard, but people are going to work hard anyway! The freedom that this business offers people is unlike almost any other kind out there, and anybody can have that lifestyle if they will just focus and put in the effort. People let the first sign of rejection shut them down. I had to share the story of the dream stealers that challenged us along the way, and how we laughed at them now and their lack of vision. There was the lady next door, the high school friend Dave called, and even my mentor from South Dakota who left our company and tried to take our organization to another company. Telling my story at that packed Opryland Hotel, I mentioned the way it would feel to pull up in the driveway of those dream stealers, rev up the motor of my car, honk the horn, and call out their name over and over again—Oh Sally! I had the entire audience chanting the names of the people who had taken their steam at a time when they had dreams so big. Don't let anybody steal your dream, and definitely don't let their lack of interest steal your belief in what you are doing.

When Dave took the stage he was given an award named after a young kid who survived a jet-ski accident that had almost claimed his life. As the president of the company came out on stage, he told the young kid's the story of courage and persistence in the face of defeat, and of the history of the award. The president then described Dave Pitcock as the person in our company with the most courage who had overcome tragedy and adversity, and yet agreed to continue to conquer his fears. He said that Dave's persistence and his dream to continue to live life and achieve the dreams that were somewhere deep inside of him had earned him this annual award. It was an awesome moment. Dave spoke about what it took to reach the top level and to earn this award. At the end of our speech, not only did our children stand next to us on stage, but all fifteen of our leaders stood with us also. It was the greatest feeling in the world to have our family, our friends, and my little Kali asleep in the arms of my uncle who had been one of our naysayers for many years. That night my uncle and his wife were one of our fifteen stars! Brooklyn and Chance held our hands as we recognized our leaders who had what it took to get the job done. Even then, it was all about recognizing our leaders.

While attending an event, I heard a quote about recognition and it is so true.

"Babies will cry for it, grown men will die for it." I believe that it is all about the way we recognize the people. Think about people in our groups, our classrooms, our churches, our communities, and even the children in our homes. It is about earning your star on the chart, hearing your name called out, or even the applause of one or two people who are proud of what you have done. We are goal-striving machines. When we look at where we are, where we are going, and what it will take to get there, it is the trophy that we keep focused on during the journey to the top. The trophy could be the satisfaction of doing it for yourself or doing it for someone who means more to you than you mean to yourself. The trophy is your focus—the reasons that drive you are your own. Imagine the feeling when you cross the finish line!

At this point in our business, we would never have to work again. Dave and I had achieved more financial independence than we had ever dreamed possible, and we had leaders that would take the business to the next level without us. We had dreamed of this day. Although a vacation sounded good, we couldn't imagine a day without being involved in the business in some way. We loved what we were doing. When you find something you love that much, you will never resent your work for the remainder of your life.

I wish I had known then that someday I would empower others and change their lives through the lessons and losses I had experienced along the way. It would have made it a lot easier to bear the disappointments, setbacks, and the embarrassments and failures I endured if I had known then that it was all part of the plan. Today I understand that advice is easier to give than it is to take when you are on the receiving end and struggling. Trust me, you will look back on everything you go through and find some good in it. Even tragedies that you can't understand at the time will help you grow stronger as a person and prepare you for the next chapter in your life. If I didn't believe this, I am not sure where I would be today. Every day of my life I thank God for my childhood, the relationships, and the lessons He has taught me, preparing me to be the person He will use during the time I am here on this earth. God has a plan for each and every one of His children. No matter what a person's past is, no matter what their family history is, or the challenges they face in their current situation, He has a plan. It isn't always easy to trust and have faith that there is good in store, but if there was one thing I could leave here on this earth when my time is up, it is this advice:

Learn that you are worthy, and no matter what your name, your nationality, or your race is, you are a champion. We are all children of a championship bloodline. We are all children of a Father who loves us, whether our birth parents are together or not. It doesn't matter what mistakes we have made, they were all paid for the day that God sacrificed his one and only Son for us. Each day is a new day and we have a clean slate to start over. God wouldn't put a dream in our hearts that we could not achieve, and to do nothing with the dream means that we do not have faith in Him and the gifts He has blessed us with. Go after your wildest dreams. Make commitments and set deadlines as if your time here is short and you have to accomplish everything on your list.

As I tell my own children, never go to bed angry and finish each day like it might be your last. Love everyone around you—regardless of what they have done that might have hurt you. I have learned the hard way about the word "regret," and I hope you never experience that feeling. The only way to be sure that you won't have regrets is to take action and follow your dreams with a belief that they will all come true. Do it even when they seem so silly. See your name in the lights! You were destined for greatness!

I know that not everyone will always be in agreement with me, and many will argue with my opinion on certain views or advice that I might give. We all have differences of opinions, but I feel we must share what we believe. I do know this: God has blessed me abundantly for everything I have given, and I will continue to give of myself. We must share the knowledge that we gain over the years in order for others to benefit from the lessons we learn. I have had hardships and pain; however, I am thankful for all that I have endured.

I believe God put the telling of my story in my heart so that I could give hope and encouragement to others. As your own experiences bring you through times of challenge and joy, remember that your life is like a movie taking you through the chapters that will reveal your destiny, as long as you just don't give up. My story is full of many ups and downs that made me stronger and allowed me to become not only successful, but happy. I hope my story impacts you in a positive way, giving you the courage to persevere, and that you find success and happiness in your life.

Afterword

SINCE THE TIME THIS BOOK WAS WRITTEN and the day Dave and Barb were recognized in Nashville, Tennessee as the company's "Top Producer," a lot has changed. It has been almost a decade and they have not only lived their dreams, but started many new ventures. Today Barb is a nationally known speaker and has inspired crowds of thousands of people to break through and achieve their dreams.

The name of her company is Barb Pitcock Unlimited, Inc. She can be reached at 785.445.3618. You can view her website at www.barbpitcock.com. Be sure to sign up for the free e-zine to continue to learn from Barb and receive inspiration on a weekly basis.

In 2009 Barb started a foundation for troubled teens and today she gives back to a cause. She knows from her own life experiences what teens need to make a change to create a difference in their lives. See the foundation at www.invisibleangels.org.
A portion of all book sales supports this foundation.

In 2010 Cindy celebrated her 15th Mother's Day since the year Chance was born. She always imagined herself seeing her grandkids graduate and dancing at their weddings. She believed she would be healed, and after the surgeries and treatments were complete, she was cancer-free—regardless of the fact that it was in her lymph nodes and statistically the reports were not good. Statistics are for people who do not have any faith. There is always someone out there that can change the outcome of what is normal expectancy. Cindy, Dave's mother, is an overcomer and an incredible grandmother and mom.
Today my mother, Lana Zorn, has become very successful and owns many businesses and real estate properties because of her ability to rise above adversity and follow her dreams, even if she was a single mom. She is my hero when I think of the one person who has

taught me that "true happiness is when you love what you do—you never work a day in your life." She is a proud grandmother of not only my three, but ten others and the number is growing every year, as my younger brothers and sisters are now grown and have families of their own. To this day, she has never stopped working and continues to look for the next project she can start or invest in.

With children in middle school and high school, I look back over the past twelve years and they went so fast I can hardly remember my children being small. I am grateful to this industry that although I was a busy mom of three, I had the vehicle to achieve freedom and experience so many "dreams come true" while my children were small. I have worked hard to instill in them the belief that they can accomplish any goals that they can dream of, and they make me very proud in everything they do. Brooklyn is a junior in high school, Chance is a sophomore, and Kali Anne is in 8th grade this year. I have to believe that this industry has taught them how to help others, to give back, and to receive abundantly—and also that it is okay to be wealthy, while you remain humble and give generously. Our children remember where we came from, and that we will never forget our family history.

Over the years my father and I have rekindled our relationship and I see him at least once a year. He has remarried and lives in South Dakota.

We are surrounded by family that lives in Russell, including all of my siblings and our mothers. Dave's dad lives just a few miles down the road from us, and today he has conquered the alcohol addiction that used to have hold of him. It has been eight years, and for that I am so proud of him.

In 2006 my best friend and business partner, David Pitcock, looked at me and said, "I want to come out of retirement and create a legacy. We've lived our dreams, and now we must allow other people to achieve theirs in the way that we were blessed." Today my husband David is the CEO and president of a company that did over one million dollars in sales in its first five months of business. He has truly changed the lives of thousands of people with his story and his vision that we could become successful in network marketing and in life. There were times when I had doubt that I could achieve my dreams, but there was never a time that I wasn't dreaming. We have been through so much together and that has made us stronger, wiser, and closer. Together we have a mission, and that is to help others live their dreams and achieve their goals with a home-based business.